7/13/88

Skip Wong

Ecclesiastes
12:12-14

Telephone Magic

H. Skip Weitzen

President, Foresight and Planning
Annapolis, Maryland

Telephone
Magic □ How to Tap

the Phone's Marketing Potential

in Your Business

McGraw-Hill Book Company

New York   St. Louis   San Francisco   Auckland   Bogotá
Hamburg   Johannesburg   London   Madrid   Mexico
Montreal   Milan   New Delhi   Panama   Paris
São Paulo   Singapore   Sydney
Tokyo   Toronto

Library of Congress Cataloging-in-Publication Data

Weitzen, H. Skip.
  Telephone magic.
  Includes index.
  1. Telephone in business.   2. Direct marketing.
I. Title.
HF5541.T4W45   1987   658.8′4   86-2856
ISBN   0-07-069124-X

1234567890   DOC/DOC   8932109876

ISBN 0-07-069124-X

*Examples given in the book of products, services, or individuals are
not intended as endorsements in any way and serve only for
illustrative purposes.*

The editors for this book were Martha Jewett and Barbara B. Toniolo,
the designer was Naomi Auerbach, and the production supervisor
was Sally Fliess. It was set in Baskerville by Braun/Brumfield, Inc.

Printed and bound by R. R. Donnelley & Sons Company.

This book is dedicated to the memory of Jonathan Coe.
His battle against death has taught me
more about life.

ABOUT THE AUTHOR

H. Skip Weitzen is president of Foresight and Planning, the
Annapolis, Maryland, consulting firm specializing in
electronic marketing applications. As an adjunct professor,
Mr. Weitzen teaches the first electronic marketing course at
The University of Maryland University College. His
extensive marketing experience includes coordination of the
media and marketing efforts in 153 cities for the Robert
Schuller organization during the building of their famous
Crystal Cathedral. He has also developed telecommunications
and marketing programs for a wide range of clients,
including businesses, service organizations, colleges, health-
care professionals, nonprofit and religious organizations.

Contents

Preface

DIAL ITEM: On September 27, 1985, the worst hurricane of the century struck the east coast of the United States. The National Weather Service set up a Hurricane Hotline. For 50 cents, people dialed 1-900-410-6622 to follow the location, movement, and strength of Hurricane Gloria, 24 hours a day.

DIAL ITEM: Mutual of Omaha, prospecting for sales agents nationwide, placed commercials on cable channel WTBS. A toll-free telephone number on the screen was the point of contact to receive more information on the career opportunity.

DIAL ITEM: Quaker Oats combined an 800 number in a sweepstakes campaign for their ready-to-eat cereal Cap'n Crunch. Twenty-four million kids called in and Cap'n Crunch's share of the cereal market increased by 30 percent over a 5-month period.

DIAL ITEM: A woman in Palm Springs, California, discovered an old painting in her attic. She called Telepraisal in Roslyn, New York. Over the phone she described the picture and gave the name of the artist. In a matter of seconds, Telepraisal gave her the painting's most recent appraised value.

DIAL ITEM: Dial-A-Shuttle was a special telephone link set up by AT&T allowing people on earth to hear astronauts talking in space. Over 1,200,000 callers listened in during a *Challenger* flight.

DIAL ITEM: A multilanguage synthesized-voice public telephone tells callers in English, Spanish, Tagalog (a language spoken in the Philippines), and two Chinese dialects, Mandarin and Cantonese, how to use the phone.

DIAL ITEM: Surrounded by Cuban forces in Grenada, a soldier used a public telephone to save a U.S. Army unit. His phone call to Ft. Bragg was placed by credit card. Officers at Ft. Bragg responded by sending in AC-130 Spectre gunships to scatter the Cubans and relieve the unit.

The telephone is changing the way business is conducted. As technology is integrated into business functions, entrepreneurs and corporations are creating new applications for the telephone within the marketing mix. Now, for the first time, *Telephone Magic* documents and defines the marketing mix of the Information Age (see Figure 1).

The marketing mix represents the synergistic effect of promotion, advertising, prospecting, sales, research, services, products, distribution, pricing, and packaging. The telecommunications technology is being absorbed into the marketing mix to produce a more efficient and value-enhancing way to satisfy the needs of the marketplace.

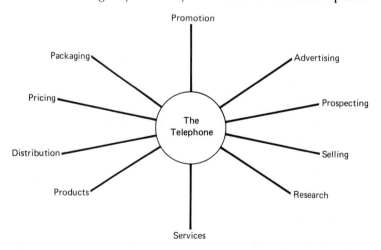

Figure 1. The Information Age marketing mix. *(Copyright © 1985 by Foresight and Planning.)*

Since the break-up of AT&T emphasis has been placed on the new telecommunications companies and their products. Yet very little attention has been paid to how the telephone is changing the way people do business. *Telephone Magic* is a point of reference for businesses as they reconsider their marketing futures. It will help you discover and tap the phone's marketing potential in your business. This book documents new telephone applications and shows how they are transforming businesses and lifestyles. After reading *Telephone Magic,* you'll never think of the telephone in the same way again.

Acknowledgments

This book could never have been written without the assistance of hundreds of entrepreneurs and corporations. They have graciously shared their creative telephone applications—the successes and failures. They are the ones who must take credit for changing the world of business. I want to take this opportunity to acknowledge two telephone pioneers: Alexander Graham Bell, who created "instant communications" because he had the courage to do something different; and William McGowan, whose tenacity and convictions opened the doors to a deregulated world of telecommunications. A special acknowledgment is also owed to AT&T for its role in making these applications possible.

There are several people who deserve special thanks for this book: Fred Southard, president of the U-Haul Corporation (now vice president of finance, Robert Schuller Ministries), for introducing me to the dynamics of the marketing mix. Over the years Fred provided me with insights and feedback that have proved invaluable in researching this subject; John Groman, senior vice president of Epsilon Data Management, for demonstrating over and over again the importance of integrating the information and communications technology into the corpoate marketing effort; Bruce McBrearty, president of Campaign Marketing Group, for sharing his insights in pioneering the paperless telemarketing center; and Jim Williams, president of the Williams Inference Service, for helping me see the early signs of business and technological change through his environmental and inferential scanning service.

I want to acknowledge and thank these marketers and businesspersons who have influenced my thinking over the years: Paul Hall, Carl Hermann, Charlie Jones, Phil Sheats, Mike Gretschel, Robert Pollero, and Bob Merkle, Anita Schmied, David W. Hearne, Gary Medovich, Arnold Chase, Paul Hawken, Jim Webb, Cecil Munsey, Al Ries, Jack Trout, John Finn, John Durkin, Fred Weitzen, Jr., Dick Disraeli, Robert Schuller, Bill Underwood, Fielding Yost, Gordon MacPherson, Adrian de la Torre, Bob Kraning, Tom Whitelock, Gary Bowman, Ron Ballard, Keith Heerman, Dick Dresselhaus.

I am grateful to my editor at McGraw-Hill, Martha Jewett. She is a true professional. Her encouragement and support kept me organized and on time. Thanks for believing in the idea.

I want to express my appreciation to the following people who reviewed various parts of the manuscript: Fred Weitzen, Sr., Laura Hess Watts, Paul Elliot, Tom Basil, Marshall Steele, Kim Coolbaugh, Melinda Bettencourt, Ron Holden, Seymour Rubin, Paul Thompson, and David Jamison. Special thanks to Wes Harty for inviting me to his writers' conference in 1977.

I'd like to acknowledge three special people whose words of affirmation were like oxygen to my lungs: Evelyn Peters, Arlene Weitzen, and Virginia Whitelock. And eternal thanks to my weekly prayer warriors, who for 3 years have encouraged me in my work, Jay Mitchell, Mike Moriarty, Eric Coolbaugh, Neil Hansberger, Tom Meekins, John Odean, John Burris, Alan Baker, and Pierre Tullier.

A special thanks to my daughters Jessica and Cassandra for praying that their daddy's dream would come true. And most importantly, this book could never have been written without the love and understanding of my wife, Julia. She had the faith to believe in me and the patience to survive the broken computer, the boxes and boxes of articles, and the publishing deadlines. Thank you.

Special Acknowledgment

The idea for this book started several years ago with a meeting in the Annapolis office of the Williams Inference Service, a business intelligence organization that monitors more than 150 newspapers and trade journals in search of early indicators of business, technological, and social changes. David Jamison, a reader-researcher with the service, pulled out a box of clippings and said to me, "Take a look at these and see what people are doing with the telephone." He handed me scores of creative telephone applications. As I read through the clippings, it struck me that I was looking at bits and pieces of a technologically enhanced marketing mix.

Since that first meeting, Mr. Jamison has provided me with several hundred newspaper and magazine articles indicating changes in how business is conducted because of the telephone. This input has been invaluable in structuring the marketing mix of the Information Age.

Introduction

How to Tap the Phone's Marketing Potential

We all face changes. The goal of *Telephone Magic* is to help you understand the new environment and the forces that are bringing about these changes. This understanding will enable you to successfully integrate the Information Age technologies and techniques into your marketing mix. Reading and applying the ideas in this book will increase your chances of opening up new markets, finding ways of creating new products and services, and generating revenue opportunities which can make the difference between earning a profit and just breaking even.

HOW TO KEEP UP WITH CHANGE

William McGowan, president of MCI Communications, perhaps better than anyone typifies the saying, "Peruse it or lose it." The office of this chief executive officer is filled with periodicals and tabloids. Business reports spill over onto window ledges and bookcases. Around the room are found stacks of newspapers, popular magazines, technical journals, and scientific papers.

Although McGowan has always been an insatiable reader, these days he believes he must ingest all available information about the new business revolution in progress. Newspapers and magazines highlight the experiences and lessons of other companies and industries which may directly affect his company or business environment.

One of the qualities that distinguishes successful executives is their ability to think fast and stay ahead of economic, social, political, and technological conditions of the environment in which they operate. Executives skilled in planning and charting a course through the dangers and opportunities of various environments are in high demand. The complexity and importance of these tasks have been amplified over the past decade because of the rapid and unpredictable changes in the environment.

As we enter the Information Age, the cost of misdirection and nondirection is high. Because events like oil cartels, grain embargos, nuclear accidents, and antitrust suits are delivered at random, the environment is almost unpredictable.

Perusing a wide variety of periodicals and tabloids provides a method for coping with external social, economic, and technical issues that may be difficult to observe or predict. Perusing helps identify emerging technologies, like the telephone, which affect the environment.

The question of what to read depends on those events that have an impact on your business. The first step is to assess carefully which issues may affect your immediate environment. Next, set your reading priorities by determining what you'll read and when. Once these steps have been completed, your next task is to obtain the vital information in a timely and organized manner. Pertinent information can be found in newspapers, magazines, reports and other publications, at trade shows, and by listening to people.

The telecommunications industry is exploding with products and publications. One way to grasp the trends of the technologies and services is to subscribe to industry periodicals and newsletters. The following is a partial list of telecommunication publications:

Teleconnect　　　(monthly)　$15/yr.
12 W. 21st St.
New York, New York 10010

Communications News　　　(monthly)　$18/year
124 S. First St.
Geneva, Illinois 60134

Tele—The Communications Magazine for Business　　　(monthly)　$29.97/year
202 N Peterborough
Peterborough, New Hampshire 03458-1194

Telephone Angles   (monthly) $65/year
P.O. Box 633
West Hartford, Connecticut 06102

Telecommunications Product Review   (monthly) $39/year
P.O. Box 128
Gaithersburg, Maryland 20877

Telephone Engineer and Management   (biweekly) $16/year
12. S. First St.
Geneva, Illinois 60134

Telephone News   (weekly) $197/year
7315 Wisconsin Ave., Suite 1200-N
Bethesda, Maryland 20814

Telephony   (monthly) $20/year
55 E. Jackson Blvd.
Chicago, Illinois 60604

Telemarketing   (monthly) $39/year
17 Park St.
Norwalk, Connecticut 06851

Laser Focus with Fiberoptic Communication   (monthly) $30/year
1001 Watertown St.
Newton, Massachusetts 02165

Business Communications Review   (bimonthly) $78/year
800 Enterprise Dr.
Oak Brook, Illinois 60521

Communication Age   (monthly) $23/year
55 E. Jackson Blvd.
Chicago, Illinois 60604

Telecommunications Week   (weekly) $28/year
National Press Bldg.
Washington, D.C. 20045

Studies have been done on how executives and managers obtain their key decision-making information. Several observations can be made from the reports: Management must rely on people inside and outside their corporation for input. Important information often comes from unexpected and remote sources: conversations on airplanes, a chance meeting with an old schoolmate, or a chat with a golf partner. Key inputs also come from subordinates who themselves need the resources to improve their knowledge. Many executives try to minimize their reliance on internal reports and meetings for their strategic input.

Top executives have their own intelligence networks for gathering data. These networks often provide the critical decision-making information. Networking introduces allies and opens up a new way of thinking about business. It provides information, feedback, techniques, advice, leads, referrals, and moral support.

Networking is a link to an ever-expanding communications community. Because a company can no longer look to a sole source—Ma Bell— for total start-to-finish assistance with telephone services and related products, networking will become vital to the success of any venture.

Part of any company's Roladex card file should be the names of participants in telecommunications societies and associations. These groups have become vital because of the importance of the telecommunications industry. The last 2 decades of the twentieth century are to the telecommunications industry what the last 2 decades of the nineteenth century were to the steel industry. To further illustrate this point, the Industrial Revolution gave America its muscle. Now the Telecommunications Revolution is giving America a finely tuned nervous system.

Speaking for the entire telecommunications industry is the United States Telephone Association (USTA). It is part of the infrastructure of telecommunications policy, representing most of the 1500 independent phone companies in the United States.

United States Telephone Association
1801 K St., NW, Suite 1201
Washington, D.C. 20006

The Society of Telecommunications Consultants is comprised of telecommunications consultants who provide technical and management expertise to business and industry. Telecommunications consultants plan telecom systems, oversee equipment specifications, monitor costs for equipment and installation, and train personnel.

The requirements for membership in the Society of Telecommunications Consultants include:

- Training, education, and/or experience in applying the knowledge and skills of telecommunications consulting
- Active employment in the profession of telecommunications consulting
- Financial and organizational independence of any organization which manufactures, distributes, or sells any telecommunications equipment, device, or transmission

Society of Telecommunications Consultants
One Rockefeller Plaza, Suite 1410
New York, New York 10020

The Association of Long Distance Telephone Companies represents long-distance carriers that compete with AT&T. They are an information clearinghouse, providing information to businesses about their members.

Association of Long Distance Telephone Companies
2000 L St., NW
Washington, D.C. 20036

The International Teleconferencing Association is a clearinghouse for teleconferencing users and suppliers. This is a good resource to contact when considering teleconferencing.

International Teleconferencing Association
P.O. Box 3706
Tysons Corner Branch
McLean, Virginia 22103

The North American Telecommunications Association members build and sell telecommunications equipment that can be connected to the Bell System.

North American Telecommunications Association
511 Second Street, NE
Washington, D.C. 20002

Exposure to literature, people, and trade shows is likened to a farmer turning the soil to make the land ready for seed. The seeds are the new ideas or technologies that may become an integral part of your company. Your harvest will be an increased market share, or a reduction of costs, or a rise in profits.

One strategic source from which to gain new insights into the applications of the telecommunications technologies is your competition. Competitive intelligence is vital to staying ahead. Start by assuming that your competitors know all your plans. Now try to get into their shoes while they are studying their business plans. Start tracking their data and try to predict their next step. Are they targeting new markets? Increasing penetration into existing markets? Pulling out of marginal or unprofitable markets? Are they implementing new telecommunications technologies or techniques to achieve any of the above objectives?

The well-managed competitive intelligence program watches the competition's share of the market, pricing structure, sales force size, organizational practices, advertising and promotion expenditures, and new equipment and technology acquisitions.

Once a market-by-market strategic plan for the competition is constructed you can determine the resources and technologies required to grow in a market, predict the most likely responses from your major competitors, and identify your competition's level of commitment to markets and market strategies.

HOW TO CREATE NEW TELEPHONE APPLICATIONS

Problems in life are a sure thing. Success is a by-product of solving your customers' problems. In many cases the key to solving problems is to view them in new ways.

One example of innovating a technique and integrating telecommunications technology to solve a problem is known as the "electronic ball and chain misdemeanor monitoring bracelet." Being tested in Albuquerque, New Mexico to solve the problem of overcrowding in county jails, the project places digital electronic bracelets on work-release prisoners and those on probation. The bracelets are worn around the clock and transmit a digital code to a device connected to the wearer's telephone. A microprocessor monitors the phone signals via a modem. The mainframe computer at Bernalillo County can detect if the wearer strays more than 200 to 300 feet from his or her telephone. If the bracelet is tampered with, a signal is also sent to the computer. A curfew can be imposed without sending a probation officer to check on the offender.

HOW TO INTEGRATE TECHNOLOGIES AND TECHNIQUES INTO THE MARKETING MIX

Telephone Magic focuses on the innovative applications of the new telephone technology. The creativity demonstrated by entrepreneurs and corporations has brought about untold rewards for the risks they have taken in these high-technology times.

Yet practicality has its reward too. This is demonstrated by companies that have profited simply by adapting a telephone technology or a proven technique to solve a similar problem.

The starting point for integrating telecom technologies and innovative techniques into your business is to find a point of reference that determines the validity of new ideas. The emerging criterion of the Information Age is providing a new business standard by asking, "Does it do more for less?"

In other words, once the technique or technology is integrated, can more work be done for less money, using less energy and requiring less labor? If the answer is yes then the technology or technique should be considered beneficial or constructive. Its implementation should enhance the durability and quality of your product or service.

Secondary criteria might include a series of follow-up questions which can measure its impact. For example, the innovation of the technique or the integration of the technology should:

- Increase production
- Increase personnel efficiency
- Improve operations
- Improve safety
- Reduce waste

- Eliminate unnecessary work
- Reduce costs
- Improve office methods
- Improve working conditions

Even if the idea earns just a single yes from your secondary criteria, the ideas should be considered constructive and researched further. This book provides information on the means for bringing a better product or service to more people at a lower cost. Telecommunications technology is creating new ways for sellers and buyers to establish close, direct, interactive contact without regard to time or distance. The development of business-to-business direct marketing is becoming the most efficient marketing process between prime manufacturers and their ultimate corporate customers.

Business-to-business direct-response marketing joins information and education to the techniques of persuasion with vehicles that provide for immediate response or more relevant dialogue. By integrating new telecommunications techniques and technologies into the marketing mix, the roles of money, media, communications, and information systems are all being redefined. This integration is proving successful for the following reasons:

- It is cost-effective. Used at the right time, the telephone is the most cost-effective marketing tool available.
- It commands personal attention. The recipient talks to a live salesperson or a "talking" computer.
- It is responsive. An answer can be requested or a special convenience extended.
- It requires immediate attention. When the telephone rings all other activity is suspended until the call is resolved.
- It provides immediate involvement once a phone number is dialed.
- It is flexible. It can be turned on, modified, and turned off with very short notice.
- It is testable. All facets of the marketing mix can be measured. Accurate and timely data can be derived to fine tune the program.

YOUR CREATIVE TELEPHONE APPLICATION

Telecommunications is to the Information Age as oil was to the Industrial Age—the lifeblood of business. The break-up of AT&T occurred rapidly, creating confusion and problems. Necessity, as always, is the mother of invention.

As businesses awaken to the fact that expertise is not available at the drop of a hat, they will be forced to work "smarter." Analytical individuals who can solve the business problems of the phone will be called on to discern the range of issues behind what is apparently a small technical problem.

Trained telecommunications managers will play a key role in the future of the American corporation. They will be required to design and manage voice and data systems while grasping the bigger corporate picture. The phone bill will no longer be viewed as a black hole within the company. Instead these telecom managers will transform telecommunications into a profit center. Top management is calling upon the telecommunications manager to integrate telecommunications technology and techniques into the marketing mix to solve the problems of their customers.

Table 1 is a "Technologically Enhanced Marketing Mix" worksheet for your use through the remainder of the book. Each chapter is filled with techniques and technologies which you may wish to adapt to your business or operation. To use the worksheet simply record the application with its page number in the blank area. *Telephone Magic* has plenty of specific, real-life examples which are intended as thought starters—to stimulate your imagination; show you innovative, fresh approaches; and illustrate how others have taken advantage of the new opportunities and solved business problems by using the telephone. The examples are not endorsements of products, services, or individuals.

You are going to find magic within these pages. Happy reading!

TABLE 1 Technologically Enhanced Marketing Mix

Marketing Mix	Page Number	Technology/Technique
Promotion		
Advertising		
Prospecting		
Selling		
Research		
Services		
Products		
Distribution		
Pricing		
Packaging		

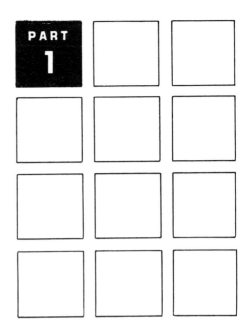

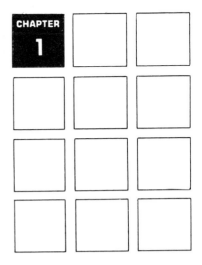
Promotion

Promotional activities are being integrated into the new technology. As telecommunications and computer technologies fuse, new promotional and public relations opportunities are being created.

Companies which are unable to afford a full-time public relations (PR) firm but which still need occasional PR help can call a telephone consultation service such as TEL-A-PR of Beverly Norman Public Relations. TEL-A-PR targets small businesses with limited public relations budgets. The service costs $15 for a 10-minute session and can be charged to a client's MasterCard or Visa account. Companies can call such a telephone consultation service to try out the PR firm before committing to a full-time contract.

INNOVATIVE PUBLIC RELATIONS

A New PR Service

By creating an independent, interactive data source for its clients, E. Bruce Harrison Company, a Washington, D.C., public relations firm, also opened up a new profit center. Harrison Information Services was started in response to a client's ongoing need for up-to-date information. This new service allowed the client to evaluate the latest developments, make policy decisions, and plan corporate actions. Now Harrison Company provides an efficient information channel between Washington, D.C. and clients' offices.

The new service adds another dimension to Harrison's standard offerings of research, information gathering, interpretation, and delivery—quicker turnaround time. This is made possible through the use of microexecutive workstations with built-in modems that "communicate" over the telephone.

Public Relations Newsroom

The 3-M Company has just introduced an electronic public relations service for journalists. The service applies electronic technology to the time-honored PR function of "kicking out press releases."

The 3-M "newsroom" allows journalists into this electronic news and feature clearinghouse through their own computers. Except for the cost of a toll call, this 3-M service is free to inquiring journalists. The 3-M newsroom is designed for the hundreds of periodical, tabloid, and broadcast writers who tap 3-M's fifty operating units for business and product stories.

Reporters using the system can ask questions, leave comments, and receive materials tailored just for them. Speed, confidentiality, and convenience benefit the journalists, any hour of the day or night. New telephone applications are increasing promotion, publicity, and public relations opportunities for companies as they integrate the new telecommunications technologies.

TELEPHONES AS THE PRODUCT IN THE PROMOTION

A unique application of the telephone in promotion was used by American Telecom. This telecommunication supplier needed a calling card that would catch distributors' attention for their new private-access branch exchange. American Telecom's PR firm brought in a retail outlet that specialized in producing chocolate forms. A chocolate telephone was produced for American Telecom's dealers.

Chocolate telephones were sent to distributors and the promotion generated a 100 percent response. It cost American Telecom $14,000 to purchase the chocolate phones and mail them to 279 independent dealers, *all* of whom expressed an interest in handling their line of products.

The cost of the mailing averaged $50 per chocolate phone, versus an average of $3.50 each for telegrams and other traditional mail campaign pieces. Yet the response rate more than offset the additional cost. The chocolate phones were preserved in the mail by packaging them in 5-pound blocks of dry ice. By the time the chocolate reached its destination, the dry ice had dissolved.

In return for its investment in capital and creativity, American Telecom successfully promoted itself in the burgeoning telecommunications equipment field.

Telephone Giveaways

With the divestiture of AT&T, competition in the telephone marketplace has become volatile. The third largest alternative long-distance telephone service, Allnet Communications Services, is showing consumers new ways to save money while offering a unique promotion.

Allnet embarked on a 60-day promotion in which telephones were given free to new subscribers. But these were not just any phones. Normally retailing for $59.95, Allnet's phones were preprogrammed to eliminate all but two of the extra numbers required as access codes before actually dialing a number. A special feature on the phone converts a rotary-dial impulse to Touch-tone signals. Newspapers nationwide carried advertisements promoting the phone offer. Television commercials also promoted the new phones.

The frill is not gone in Detroit either. Cash rebates have become passé as a lure into auto showrooms, but Detroit isn't forgetting come-ons entirely. Buick, for instance, added a $3000 car telephone for Chicago buyers of its Riviera models.

Decorator Telephones

The Sharper Image is the fastest-growing catalog in the direct-mail industry. It reaches one of every ten U.S. homes, with an average sale of $165. Founder Richard Thalheimer describes himself as having an "extremely high level of taste," being "highly intelligent," with "a true salesman's personality and a sociologist's curiosity about people." It is this combination that helps him predict the future.

Thalheimer seems to know when a trend is coming and when it is leaving. Among the trends that Thalheimer displays are telephones camouflaged as duck decoys. The selling price is $249.

This is an example of how manufacturers are redesigning the telephone. The phone has reached a stage of its development where it adds to the decor of the surroundings rather than being an unattractive necessity of modern life.

The decorator phones can be likened to stereo systems purchased in styles to match the rest of the furniture in rooms where they are located. On the outside these camouflaged phones may resemble phones of years gone by. But on the inside, advanced electronic components provide modern operational advantages.

Phone styles range from French Provincial to Mickey Mouse to a pay station phone for the home. Now Heinz 57 has turned the size and shape of its 14-ounce tomato ketchup bottle into a telephone. The push buttons are located on the bottom of the "bottle." The phone can be ordered from the Heinz Ketchup Company.

TELEPHONES TO PROMOTE PEOPLE

Promoting Record Artists

Radio listeners are no longer just tuning in—they are calling in. A new radio show has emerged that allows fans to call a toll-free number and talk to their favorite contemporary hit-recording artists. This Sunday night show is fed via digital satellite from its Los Angeles recording studio to RKO radio networks across the United States. It is hosted by Jo Interrante and Father Guido Sarducci of *Saturday Night Live* fame.

Promoting an Author

Victor Herman returned to his native United States after 45 years inside the Soviet Union. Herman is now telling about his 18 years as a Siberian exile through a new book called *Coming Out of the Ice*.

Herman traveled to Russia from Detroit in 1931 when his father agreed to help build a Ford Motor Company plant in Gorky. The Stalin purges reversed the fortunes of Mr. Herman and 300 other American Ford workers who were sent to a forced labor camp. Herman was the only survivor.

Coming Out of the Ice, recounting Herman's story, was also adapted for a TV movie. Now the book can be ordered from any phone in the world by calling 1-800-GET-BOOK. Callers are told the price, and an operator takes the credit card number over the phone. Distributors and bookstores can deliver the book anywhere in the world.

TELEPHONES TO PROMOTE THE CORPORATE EFFORT

As times change and the communications environment is altered, promotional and public relations strategies are being reexamined. When the American Express Company announced its first earnings decline in 36 years (in December, 1983), the vice president of investor relations decided against sending out the standard press releases or scheduling an analysts' meeting.

Instead, a conference call was organized between virtually all the Wall Street analysts who cover the stock and American Express executives. At 10:00 A.M. on December 12, American Express operators began dialing for the analysts. Twenty minutes later, with all the analysts on their phones, several American Express executives stood by to answer questions.

Breaking bad news can be awkward, but American Express shared its report in a unique way. Overall, the response was positive. The key to the success of the conference call was that everybody got the same message at the same time.

Now, when bad news breaks, more and more companies are responding with "damage control" programs. The purpose is to tell the full story clearly and consistently to everyone who should know: stockholders, clients, employees, the industry, and the media. The tools to convey the message in these damage control programs include press releases, letters, telex messages, interoffice memos, and the telephone for conference calls. In today's volatile marketplace, bad news needs to be dispensed as quickly and accurately as possible.

Proxy by Phone

Corporate raider Carl Icahn recently proposed to take control of the Phillips 66 Company for $4.2 billion in cash. Phillips took out full-page newspaper ads urging shareholders to take a hard look at Icahn's proposal.

Phillips urged shareholders to vote for the Phillips recapitalization plan. The ads stated "Time is growing short. Please sign, date, and mail the Phillips white proxy card or follow the Datagram procedure below. If you need further information on voting, including instructions on voting by TOLL-FREE Datagram, call Phillips toll-free at 800-431-2624." Phillips allowed shareholders to vote their shares by phone anytime, day or night.

Today, corporations are being confronted by social and political unrest. Pressure seems to be arising from two major sources: the environmental abuses from pollution and the changing values, attitudes, and behavior of consumers, employees, stockholders, and social groups.

A corporation's image can be improved when executives learn to face the facts, learn to read the early signs of trouble, and act quickly to bring corporate activities into line with reasonable public expectations, not when they try to conjure up a good story when performance fails.

Today's business environment requires that senior management develop accurate and timely consumer feedback systems. With instant communications, the promotion, publicity, and public relations departments can better recognize and deal with the public issues while still in their dormant phases. Phillips 66 Company's integration of telecommunications in their corporate promotion effort helped them perceive a trend established by corporate raiders and then act on it quickly.

Telephone Seminar Promotion

Personalized telephone follow-up used in conjunction with direct marketing can increase response rates for corporate seminars. Adding an incentive to direct mail increases the return by 8 to 15 percent. A scripted telemarketing follow-up designed to reinforce the direct-mail package and neutralize objections can boost response rates by as much as 25 percent.

Along with increasing attendance to seminars, telephone sales promotions also provide an underpinning of good feelings about the company. Telemarketing scripts can create a positive image for a company's product or service. By reinforcing past purchasing decisions, telephone promotions secure an edge in a competitive environment.

Telephone seminar promotions can double as a long-term awareness-building strategy and a short-term sales tool. The personalization of the telephone capitalizes on buyer awareness and tailors the product to the buyer's needs. When properly designed, telephone promotional support programs improve profits by accelerating the sales process and enhancing sales efficiency.

Telephones in Catalog Promotions

A survey of 182 consumer catalog companies determined the effect 800 numbers had on the promotion of catalog sales. Nearly 97 percent of the respondents who added 800 numbers to their catalogs received an increase in orders over the first 6 months. Of those, 74 percent reported an increase in the average order size over the same period.

The 800 number's ability to attract orders also increased with the number of times it appeared in the catalog. Also, the higher the average price of a catalog's items, the more likely the 800 number itself would influence the number of orders.

A toll-free number can also affect gender orders. Promotions with the 800 number pull better in male-oriented catalogs than in female-oriented catalogs.

Finally, the study noted that one-third of the respondents reported problems with the toll-free operations. In-house operations seemed to perform better than service bureaus.

Telephones in Point-of-Purchase Promotions

Telephones assist professionally conducted audits to ensure that point-of-purchase promotions are executed properly. Such an audit was performed by a national pet food marketer.

The company had invested millions of dollars in shipping and media placement. A survey found that many stores did not stock the product. A service agency was hired to monitor distribution, report out-of-stock items, and help individual stores merchandise the product.

During the promotion, distribution was carefully monitored in major markets. Within each market, auditors visited chain and large independent stores. Data from each store were immediately relayed to field sales managers. Field salespeople were notified when problem accounts were isolated from the data. Auditors then revisited the problem stores. At times, auditors even rushed to warehouses to pick up the product and place it on the shelves of the stores that were out of stock.

The success of the audit was credited to the telecommunications system. The telecommunications network and computer capabilities improved the speed and flow of information. Trained personnel provided strategic data to management within 2 days of the audit. The program was a winner.

Telecommunications will play an increasingly bigger role in nationwide promotions. Even well-planned promotions can fail because of shipping problems or organizational inadequacies. Telephone audits allow for midcourse corrections to salvage the promotions.

AT&T's Discount Promotion

Residential customers can receive discounts on airline tickets, stereos, and other goods and services, depending on the number of long-distance calls they make. These are provided by AT&T in their promotional effort.

AT&T is stepping up its battle against other providers of long-distance service such as MCI, GTE Sprint, and ITT. The program is available to customers who use their long-distance service each month.

The promotion gives $1 toward the purchase of goods and services to customers for each dollar of long-distance calling. The discounts, however, neither alter the customers' phone bills nor can they be used against their bills. Companies participating in AT&T's promotional program include Trans World Airlines, Polaroid, Levi Strauss, Avis, Amtrak, and others. The twenty-eight companies initially enrolled in the program are, in effect, absorbing the cost of the discounts in exchange for the additional sales.

Of AT&T's 80 million residential long-distance customers, 25 million with average bills of $11 or more were automatically enrolled in the plan. Packets explaining the discount program were mailed to these customers.

Promoting a New Image

The U.S. Postal Service, whose corporate image has been under attack for gross inefficiencies and poor service, took a giant step forward to remedy this situation. By integrating a toll-free line from 7:30 A.M. to 8:00 P.M. EDT, the Postal Service allows callers to obtain zip code numbers by phone. A caller dials 1-800-228-8777, gives the street address and city, then receives the appropriate zip code from the operator.

The U.S. Postal Service Consumer Advocate's office in Washington, D.C. has also installed a telecommunications device to help deaf customers who want to call in with inquiries or complaints about their mail service. Any hearing-impaired person who has access to a telecommunications device for the deaf (TDD) may call 1-202-245-3858 to communicate with a USPS consumer representative by means of a TDD in postal service headquarters. This is good public relations and may prove helpful for some of America's 8 million hearing-impaired citizens.

TELEPHONES TO PROMOTE GLOBAL RELATIONS

The British Broadcasting Corporation (BBC) promoted Margaret Thatcher as the first prime minister to take part in a global phone-in. The radio phone-in was once considered a low-key, local affair that radio people used as a cheap way to fill airtime. But in October, 1983, Prime Minister Thatcher made radio talk-show history.

Out of a radio audience of up to 100 million, a dozen fortunate callers spoke to Mrs. Thatcher. All phone lines into the London studio were jammed with calls from every continent except Antarctica for nearly 2 hours before the program aired.

The prime minister's decision to participate in the phone-in was courageous. The program was aired live and there was no lead time on the questions coming in.

As it happened, Mrs. Thatcher spoke to the world on the weekend following America's intervention in Grenada. A caller from neighboring Barbados asked why, with her known opposition to communism, she had failed to act decisively there. Her reply made the headlines of every British newspaper the next day.

Dial-a-Shuttle

A special telephone line was set up so people could listen to astronauts talking in the space shuttle *Challenger* prior to its tragic last flight. It drew more than 241,000 callers during its first 2 days. Dial-a-Shuttle, introduced in 1980 by AT&T, could handle up to 8000 calls a minute and operated throughout the flight. In the United States listeners dialed 1-900-410-6272. It cost 50 cents for the first minute and 35 cents for each additional minute plus tax.

Back on earth there were irritation and large phone bills. Callers were surprised to find advertisements on the line when they had paid to listen to astronauts. The 30-second ads were cycled in every 5 minutes thanking Tang, American Airlines, and Quality Inns for their sponsorship of the phone-in program.

One woman in Austin, Texas, not realizing that the call cost money, dialed the number at night. She left the phone off the hook so her son could listen in when he awoke in the morning. Her phone bill amounted to over $200. "You would think for $200 we would at least get to talk to one of them," she complained.

Promoting Third-World Development

The telephone is seen as a key technology in promoting development and global cooperation in third-world countries such as Malaysia, Egypt, Sri Lanka, and China.

Malaysia. In the jungles and mountainous terrain of Malaysia, it is difficult to lay cables for a telephone system. Ericsson Radio Systems of

Sweden has agreed to supply Malaysia with a completely automatic cellular telephone system. Within a decade Ericsson will hook up 50,000 mobile phones. In many cases, radio phones are Malaysia's only means of communication with the outside world.

Egypt. The University of Cairo and the Massachusetts Institute of Technology assessed the benefits of a telephone to 146 Egyptian villages at 36 times its cost to the user. This was calculated only on the basis of the time saved. With other related savings added in such as the amount of business lost if no phone was available, the benefits of the telephone worked out to 85 times its cost.

Sri Lanka. In Sri Lanka, the World Bank reported that when telephones were installed in several villages, farmers began selling their produce at 85 percent of its price in Colombo. Prior to the phone installation, produce was selling at 55 percent of the Colombo price.

China. The personal telephone is a status symbol in China. Literally translated as "electric words," a phone is one of the Chinese economy's scarcest commodities. With just 3 million phones for a billion people, officials in China acknowledge that the nation has a long way to go to match the Asian average of one phone for every thirty-three people.

Improved Productivity

In developing countries, the measurable impact of the telephone on economic development is significant. American researchers from the Brookings Institution, University of Texas, and Stanford University showed that a 1 percent rise in the number of telephones per 100 people between 1950 and 1955 (in fifty-two countries studied) contributed to a rise in per capita income between 1955 and 1962 of about 3 percent.

SUMMARY

No one likes to be criticized. But many companies are becoming more willing to listen to criticism in light of research findings: The majority of unhappy customers do not complain to the company. They simply switch brands, then complain about their bad experience to their friends.

It's been found that consumers don't complain for three reasons:

1. It's too much trouble.

2. It's difficult to find someone to complain to.
3. Why bother when nothing is going to happen anyway?

Companies are making it easier for consumers to communicate their criticisms. This is helping to build a positive public image and retain customer loyalty. Telephone hot lines are being installed to break through consumer cynicism and treat customers in a more personalized manner.

Corporations benefit in other ways by promoting their hot lines:

• Direct communications allow a company to determine consumer complaints quicker than by written correspondence.

• Consumer complaints and inquiries have significant marketing implications. New product ideas can be inferred from personal feedback.

• Adding a toll-free number on new products in test markets helps a company gain immediate feedback of consumer attitudes toward the new products.

• With half of all consumer problems relating to product misuse, 800 numbers give companies feedback on product directions.

• Studies show that companies are likely to reduce product liability up to 80 percent by simply giving the consumer someone to talk to via an 800 number.

The success of telephone hot lines comes in making a large company seem personal. Proctor and Gamble has listed its toll-free numbers on its products since 1974. In 1984, it answered more than 430,000 product-related questions. Hot-line questions and complaints are generally filed and studied by marketing executives and product managers.

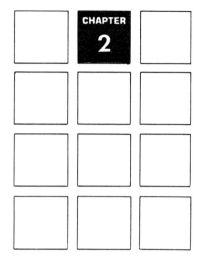

Advertising

The key to successfully integrating the telephone into your advertising is knowing what you expect your advertising to do:

- Bring in new customers
- Upgrade occasional users into regular customers
- Keep competition away
- Upgrade the dollar volume per purchase
- Cross sell other products or services

Once you decide what you need to communicate, then you can test the technologies and techniques that best communicate your message. One example is that of Fly Faire.

Servicing independent travel agents, Fly Faire packages are described on recorded messages. They received 2000 phone calls on the first day the ad appeared.

Each phone number is devoted to a prerecorded description of a specific vacation package offered by Fly Faire. A special number plays a taped message explaining the benefits of booking a vacation through an independent travel agent.

Fly Faire positions itself against the competition by providing more contact with the public for longer periods of time. Fly Faire information is available to the public 24 hours a day, 7 days a week.

TELEPHONE NUMBERS AS ADVERTISING

Alpha translations are phone numbers that spell out the names of companies, their products, or services. With 1.4 billion alpha translations available through 179 separate exchanges, the possibilities are almost endless.

Greg Griswold of Madison, Wisconsin owns the legal rights to 1300 toll-free phone numbers, representing the names or logos of well-known American firms. For his ownership, Griswold pays AT&T and local telephone operating companies about $15,000 each month.

There is no conclusive data to suggest that these numbers outperform easy-to-remember regular numbers. Yet companies who have them say they work. A coalition of nuclear-freeze groups used Griswold's 800-NUCLEAR to build its mailing list after the ABC television movie *The Day After* was shown in 1983. Results: 120,000 calls in a 3-week period.

1-800-FLOWERS

The growing importance of alpha translations is highlighted in the trademark infringement suit by Felly's Flowers against 1-800-FLOWERS. Al Felly has been growing and selling flowers for 35 years. In the 1970s he filed federal trademark papers for both 1-800-FLOWERS and 1-800-FLORIST.

At the time, with the Bell System computer's limitations, numbers could only be assigned sequentially. So in 1982, Felly was notified that he could only get 1-800-FLORIST. Consequently, Curtis Jahn, owner of a trucking and warehousing company, was assigned the number 1-800-FLOWERS.

Enter venture capitalist Bill Alexander. Realizing the value of alpha translations, Alexander dialed 1-800-FLOWERS. In 1983, Alexander and Jahn started a florist operation based on the number. The infringement suit by Felly charges that Curtis Jahn's florist operation is damaging Felly's own reputation in the industry.

In 1982, sales from wire orders through retail florists produced $725 million of their $3 billion in volume. Bill Alexander figures that 1-800-FLOWERS could earn his venture $400 million per year.

Number owners, however, cannot spell out numbers in directories or with directory assistance. AT&T also states in their contracts that any potential 800 customer must not advertise the number or its translation until it is in service.

714-NEW-HOPE

The most common personal problems include anxiety, depression, and loneliness. Distressed and lonely people generally have nobody to talk with about their troubles. As a result they suffer deeply from a sense of isolation and alienation from other people.

To solve this problem, New Hope was opened on September 15, 1968, at the Garden Grove Community Church. It became the first 24-hour-a-day telephone counseling-crisis intervention service in the United States to be sponsored by a single church. Crisis situations can happen anytime, so the New Hope counselors are available 7 days a week, all hours of the day. A volunteer staff of over 300 trained and committed people work at the New Hope Counseling Center.

Since 1968, New Hope has received nearly half a million calls, averaging about 6000 calls each month. However, it was not always clear that the phone number would be such a "North Star" for people who hurt. It was founding pastor Dr. Robert Schuller's goal to communicate the message of hope in the number. When the combination of digits that spell *new hope* would not fit the exchange of the Garden Grove Telephone Company, Schuller did not give up. He went to Orange County and for a small fee of $26 the phone company helped him establish the New Hope Telephone Counseling Service. Over the years, 1-714-NEW-HOPE has been one of the most easily recognized and remembered telephone numbers in the counseling field.

900-210-BURT

Burt Reynolds's fans were dialing 900-210-BURT for 2 weeks between December 5 and December 18, 1983. Everyone who made the 50-cent telephone call heard Burt Reynolds talk about his new movie *The Man Who Loved Women*. Creative advertising of the movie tied the spelling of Reynolds's first name into the telephone promotion.

TELEPHONES AS THE ADVERTISING MEDIUM

Movie Promotion

The promoters of *The Man Who Loved Women* also used 900-210-BURT to advertise the movie. There was even a payoff for the callers as the telephone was turned into an advertising medium. At the end of the tape-recorded message by Burt Reynolds, listeners were given details on how they could become eligible to receive a personal phone call from Reynolds. Every caller heard Burt pitch his movie, then qualified for a contest that would link them live with the popular actor.

In 2 weeks, 93,887 people spent 50 cents to hear Reynolds advertise the movie, adding $46,943.50 to the movie promoter's coffers. Then six lucky callers were picked at random and received their live phone calls from Burt Reynolds.

People are also dialing to hear recorded telephone messages touting Broadway shows. Fans called 1-900-210-CAGE to hear selections from the Broadway musical *La Cage Aux Folles* with comments from stars George Hearn and Gene Barry.

Dial-It

The deregulated telecommunications field is creating new opportunities for smaller businesses. The FCC's decision to bar the Bell Operating Companies from providing enhanced services after January 1, 1984 opened the way for companies to sponsor announcement services. Now anyone can use the telephone as an advertising medium.

Companies like Phone Programs (New York), Communications Team (Philadelphia), and Dial-It Services (Newport, Connecticut) started bidding for the rights to the public announcement business. Phone Programs operates twelve lines for daily horoscopes in Detroit and six lines with varied services in Chicago.

These "dial-it" programs were started in 1939 by Dial-a-Forecast. Next to television and radio, Dial-a-Forecast by phone has been one of the best ways to get weather predictions distributed.

But the industry has changed. Phone companies are turning their weather and time services over to telephone entrepreneurs and commercial sponsors such as banks and corporations.

The incentive for the entrepreneur is found in the 976 prefix. The phone company bills the caller for each local call to that number. Once the phone company collects the money, they split the revenue with the message sponsor. Information handlers are expanding their use of the 976 prefix to distribute weather, sports scores, stock market quotes, quiz games, and more.

TELEPHONES AS THE ADVERTISING RESPONSE MEDIUM

A great deal of attention is being focused on getting magazine inquiries to the advertiser faster while providing more information for follow-up. *Harper's Bazaar* is now bypassing the written inquiry process.

Readers are dialing the phone to place orders. The magazine has developed a program called Pink Hotline featuring a nationwide toll-free number prominently displayed in the ads of participating advertisers. *Harper's Bazaar* has also developed a method of hooking readers up with advertisers. Readers can dial a number, reach an independent operator hired by *Harper's Bazaar,* and order merchandise via credit card.

Advertisers don't pay extra to be hooked up with the Pink Hotline. To qualify though, they must have purchased at least a quarter-page ad. Then they pay a $2.50 fee for each order placed through the hot line.

Harper's Bazaar Pink Hotline increases advertising revenues by showing their accounts that it's not too late to run Christmas ads in November and December. The hot line serves as a vehicle to capture last-minute holiday sales at a time when *Harper's Bazaar* readers are looking for merchandise.

Advertisers in *Architectural Record* are also replacing their inquiry-card responses with phone calls from readers. Advertisers can now conceivably respond to a reader inquiry within minutes. The typical turnaround time for a reader service card from a potential buyer to the seller is 6 weeks. This faster response means increased sales which in turn means more advertising for the magazine.

Paul Beatty, publisher of the McGraw-Hill publication *Architectural Record,* calls the reader-inquiry process "our most valuable sales tool." His goal is to make the magazine a more efficient marketplace for the sale of his advertisers' products. This means helping to process sales leads quicker than before.

This revolutionary computerized program to service subscribers and advertisers works by Touch-tone phone and is called the Automatic Inquiry Managment System (AIMS). With advertisers accessing the system directly to obtain the inquirers' names, immediate response can be made to the readers' requests. The advertising community views these programs with great interest, which may translate into future sales.

Direct-Response Radio

Radio carried most of the direct marketing advertising until the introduction of television. The pendulum is swinging back as advertisers search for alternative media outlets.

Radio offers the immediacy of broadcast and a specialized audience.

Certain direct-response products also lend themselves better to audio than to video presentations.

For optimal effectiveness, radio's 1-minute direct-response commercial ceiling needs to allow for a more segmented approach. A better format would intersperse commercials with programming during sponsored programs which would be about 15 minutes long. This allows listeners more opportunity to phone in for the product.

WFMT, Chicago's premier-quality FM station, feeds its signals into cable radio across the country. For a single audience participation program, it receives hundreds of calls from throughout the United States. A typical scenario begins with the phone ringing at WFMT. The call is transferred to a clerk and the caller says, "Hello, I'm calling from New Jersey, and I'd like to order some items you advertised on the radio."

The success of these programs depends on several factors:

1. Providing an easy-to-remember and frequently advertised telephone number
2. Offering listeners several chances to respond
3. Alternating rhythm of commercials and regular programming
4. Giving interested listeners the incentive to tune into the program

Infomercials

An aggressive advertising concept was introduced through the cable-TV industry. Cableshop offers an interactive display of 5- to 7-minute "infomercials." These are played on three cable channels in the test market of Peabody, Massachusetts. Each home is given a code number and a telephone listing. In the monthly listing guide, each of the twenty-one infomercials is given a number.

The success of the infomercial is due to its interactive nature, which results from a phone call. Another benefit is the infomercial's ability to generate measurable direct-response reports. Subscribers' calls create a calling record that can be analyzed for the program's strengths and weaknesses.

Financial Advertising

Deregulation of the banking industry is heating up the competition among financial services. Aggressive advertising campaigns are becoming commonplace in newspapers and trade journals. The most effective financial advertisers generally meet these five criteria in their ads:

1. Provide a direct-response vehicle such as an 800 telephone number to facilitate the implementation of the decision

2. Provide portfolio managers with decision-oriented information
3. Provide consistency with the company's investor relations programs
4. Place the information within a newsworthy context
5. Provide information not readily available from traditional sources

Pizza Delivery

Pantera's Pizza is investing $750,000 to capture the home-delivery segment of the St. Louis pizza market. The chain's thirty-eight local outlets hold 21 percent of the annual $100 million in area pizza sales, not including frozen pizza products.

Pantera's is initiating a home-delivery system to be part of a growing home-delivery trend. Nationwide, home-delivery captured 16 percent of all pizza sales in 1984 compared to 10 percent in 1979. Pantera's is investing $250,000 in advertising to accompany their home-delivery system.

The key to the system's success is found in its single phone number. Rather than have thirty-eight numbers, one for each pizza shop, Pantera's has one telephone number for home delivery. A computer system streamlines service by reducing the time that operators spend on the telephone with customers. The computer connects the telephone number given by the caller with the nearest Pantera's Pizza outlet.

Repeat customers do not even have to give their addresses because they are stored in the computer's memory. A repeat customer can be serviced in 20 seconds while a first-time customer can be helped in 45 seconds.

Pantera's projects phone activity to average 70,000 calls each month. The investment in the computer-telephone was about $400,000 for the equipment. Operating costs run about 10 cents a call or $7000 a month.

For Pantera's Pizza, telemarketing, or direct marketing by telephone, is growing quickly. Many other companies are tying 800 numbers into their TV commercials with great success. However, the use of network television for toll-free campaigns has one major drawback: It tends to cause circuit overloads during the 10-minute "burst period" following a commercial.

TELEPHONE SUPPORT ADVERTISING

The Yellow Pages

Yellow Page ads are still an invaluable part of any media mix. To use Yellow Page ads most effectively you must be able to answer the who, what, where, when, and why for potential customers.

- *Who.*   Your company name should be descriptive or already well known in order to be used in the headline. Otherwise it is more effective to use the headline to sell a feature such as a large selection or a specialty.
- *What.*   List your full range of products and services including brand names.
- *Where.*   Give the address, pinpointing the location. Mention nearby intersections, highways, and other landmarks. A map in the corner is a good idea.
- *When.*   List your hours of operation.
- *Why.*   Emphasize the special features and benefits of your company.

Bell Yellow Pages representatives can provide assistance as you develop the copy and choose your graphics.

Instant Yellow Pages

American Business Lists, Inc. of Omaha, Nebraska has entered data from the Yellow Pages of 4800 American telephone books into its computers to create its Instant Yellow Pages service. The data base of 5 million entries is cross-indexed by standard Yellow Pages categories and zip codes. A computer equipped with a modem to communicate over telephone lines is required to use this service. There is a $100 initial setup charge. After that, the cost is $90 for 6 months and $1 per minute of connect time. The names and addresses of every listing in America is now just a phone call away.

The Green Pages

With more than 2 billion calls made on 800 numbers in 1983, an Ann Arbor, Michigan, company has designed a national list of toll-free 800 telephone numbers arranged by type of business. They call it the *Green Pages.*

This 246-page volume lists 27,000 numbers that can be called toll-free. Even at $12.95, the book pays for itself in just a few calls.

AT&T Communications, a division of American Telephone and Telegraph, is also distributing toll-free 800-number directories. AT&T's toll-free business and consumer directories cost $8.75 and $6.25, respectively. Information on 800 numbers can still be obtained at no charge by calling 1-800-555-1212.

Rolodex Cards and Postcards

Two simple and effective forms of support advertising include Rolodex cards and change-of-phone-number postcards. Rolodex cards can be designed with colors or in extra large sizes so they stand out among the other cards. And now Rolodex cards can be generated from continuous-feed computer forms.

The change-of-phone-number postcards can be designed with creative graphics. This attracts attention and promotes good customer relations. By providing the new number you actually create a tool that acts as a prospecting foot-in-the-door technique.

Talk Back

Consumers can now communicate directly with an advertiser whose ads are offensive. Thomas Nelson Publishers is distributing *Talk Back*, a directory of addresses and telephone numbers of corporations that advertise on network television. The National Federation for Decency is the copyright holder. Letters of support or phone calls are encouraged if an advertiser does something meritorious.

Tele-Photo Phone Book

The *Tele-Photo Phone Book* is an emergency phone book for kids. It teaches youngsters the proper use of the phone, particularly during emergencies. The book is published by Mother Goose Distributing in Pasadena, California. Photos and drawings are used to instruct nonreaders on numbers to call in emergency situations. There are also pages for photos and phone numbers of friends.

Women's Yellow Pages

The *Greater Philadelphia Women's Yellow Pages*, entering its second year, is a publication that contains a listing of female-owned businesses in a Yellow Pages format.

The publication, which highlights women's economic clout, generated revenues of about $35,000 from its 1984 edition. With 470 advertisers, this was nearly double the 1983 total of 250 advertisers. It had a 73 percent renewal rate from advertisers.

Ten thousand copies are printed and distributed. Rates range from $45 for a listing to $420 for a full-page advertisement. There are an estimated 11,000 female-owned businesses in the Philadelphia area.

Spanish Yellow Pages

Las Pagmas Amerillas de Pacific Bell, a Spanish Yellow Pages, was introduced in 1985 for 2 million Spanish-speaking residents and 6000 Hispanic businesses in Los Angeles. Miami, with 580,000 Spanish-speaking residents, also brought out a Spanish Yellow Pages.

Children's Yellow Pages

The *Children's Yellow Pages* is 147 pages long and sold 10,000 copies in the first 2 months for $5.95 each. The book has about 3500 free listings for children and their families.

SUMMARY

One purpose of advertising is to get prospects coming to you so your salespeople can negotiate a sale. The telephone is becoming an important factor in advertising because of its measurable controls. To measure the profitability of a telephone advertising program, perform three calculations: Find the dollar value of a new customer over a particular period of time, the average annual cost of finding new customers, and the average annual profit generated by new customers.

Take these figures and set up ratios to explore the relationships between telephone advertising, sales, and sales expense. These ratios help define the range of telephone advertising as a percentage of sales expense. The next step is to find where telephone advertising spending makes its greatest impact. Once the point of maximum telephone advertising payoff is isolated, operating near that point will bring the biggest "bang for your advertising buck."

The bottom line to profitable advertising is to make the sales expense a smaller part of sales as advertising becomes a larger part of the sales expense. The telephone, when integrated into the advertising program, often lowers the cost of sales.

The starting point for improving the profitability of your advertising program is to establish a checklist. This will focus the tasks required to achieve your objectives. Every businessperson, at some time, will need to address these key issues:

- Who do you want to reach through your advertising?
- How large is your audience?
- What factors influence the buying patterns of this audience?
- What do you want to communicate to this audience?

- What media mix will provide the most cost-effective penetration for your message to this audience?
- How are you going to measure the results of your advertising effort?

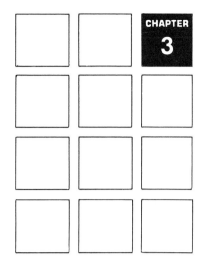

Prospecting

Sales staffs are beginning to use new prospecting devices to introduce traditional goods and services to the marketplace. Prospecting is the search for a potential customer or purchaser. These tools include telephones, computers, videocassette recorders, automatic dialers, and more.

Salespeople are trading in their product sample cases for video-disc players or compact portable computers to display their wares. Many more have given up traveling altogether to spend 8 hours a day on the phone talking to prospective customers.

The driving force behind the changes is the corporate emphasis on productivity. Top executives are pressuring sales and marketing managers to boost sales without increasing personnel. "Electronic prospecting" is cost-effective for three reasons:

1. *High Expenses.* The cost of keeping a salesperson on the road actually exceeds the salesperson's wages in some cases.
2. *Affordable Technology.* The price of using technology in

telemarketing, teleconferencing, and computerized selling has dropped significantly. The technology is now accessible for even small companies.
   3. *Innovative Techniques.* Tough competition is sparking innovation in prospecting techniques. Companies are searching for that something extra that will provide a higher rate of sales conversions from prospects.

Despite the alternatives, telephones remain the most reliable and inexpensive tool for business-to-business prospecting. For a telephone prospecting program to be successful, it needs to be addressed within the following context:

- What is prospecting's role in your marketing mix?
- What are your prospecting strategy options?
- What is your prospective account management strategy?
- What will the prospecting program cost and return in sales volume?

TARGETING PROSPECTS BY TELEPHONE

In 1984, the Republican Party began prospecting by phone for new voters to build party registration. The process started with a computer that prescreened the names and generated a list of qualified prospects. The process works this way: The list of driver's license holders is merged with registered voters. The names of those under 18 years of age or those previously registered are removed.
   The remaining list of unregistered voters with driver's licenses is then merged with the list of Democratic and Republican zip codes and precincts. This yields a list of unregistered license holders by zip codes and precincts.
   The names of those in Democratic zip codes and precincts are then removed. The remaining unregistered license holders in Republican zip codes and precincts are merged with a "metro-mail" phone list. All those not on the phone list are purged. This yields the list of prospective Republican voters: unregistered license holders in Republican zip codes and precincts who are on the metro-mail phone list.
   The telemarketing operators then call these prospects and ask three questions:

   1. "Have you registered to vote recently?" If the answer is yes the names are removed. If the answer is no they are asked the second question.
   2. "Do you expect to vote in the November election?" If the answer is

no the names are purged. If the answer is yes they are asked the third question.

3. "Will you be voting for President Reagan?" If the answer is no the names are scratched. If the answer is yes these names go on the list of qualified Republican prospects.

These qualified names receive a computer-generated personalized letter that aids in voter registration.

Instant Prospecting

The Honeywell Corporation uses an 800 number and a computerized inquiry system to cut inquiry response time and lead qualification time. To better handle direct mail and reader reply cards, Honeywell's inquiry-processing system expanded into a computer-assisted telemarketing program. The process control division established a toll-free sales hot line. Phone banks were set up in the corporate facility.

Prospects can now bypass the written inquiry reader reply device by calling Honeywell directly through the 800 number found in their ads. Individual extension numbers are linked to product and service groups.

Inquiries are handled in the following manner: Telemarketing operators enter the extension number on the videoscreen. A script appears with questions specifically keyed to the product groups and to the ad that generated the response. This actually qualifies the caller in terms of product need, size of plant, and other critical information.

With the data in computer memory, mailing labels and lists are printed and rushed overnight to the division. A literature-fulfillment house distributes the requested product information. When the customer need is immediate, the sales force is notified by electronic mail.

The prospect's phone response not only cuts inquiry response and lead qualification time but it eliminates the search for numbers on reader response cards.

Qualified Prospects

The three major goals of a prospecting strategy include:

1. Isolating which prospect needs require the purchase of the product or service
2. Giving the prospect a good reason to buy
3. Closing the sale by helping the customer see how the product or service solves the problem

Few companies are as effective in fulfilling these three functions as the Xerox Corporation. Once Xerox isolates a market for its products, they establish a strategy for reaching prospective customers. The growth of their computer service retail outlets is part of a new marketing effort. A recent Xerox prospecting effort targeted manufacturers with revenues under $10 million in need of a microcomputer system. Only about 5 percent of the 40,000 to 50,000 companies with under $10 million per year in revenues have a computer powerful enough to automate their businesses.

Xerox's strategy involves telemarketing and direct mail to bring twenty to twenty-five people into their retail centers for a product seminar. Each seminar yields about six to eight serious prospects and serves as a replacement for the initial sales call.

Following the seminar, a salesperson and often a consultant are sent to the qualified prospect's manufacturing plant. This strategy is producing a high ratio of new accounts per month for each retail outlet.

Telecomputer Prospecting

Telecomputer prospecting is growing in popularity. An ad reads, "Get hot leads without spending a minute on the phone. All you have to do is sell." Computer dialers can generate an abundance of leads each day while the sales force is away from the office. Here's how it works.

When someone answers the phone at the other end, the computer dialer introduces "itself." Most people listen because they have never held a conversation with a computer before.

If the prospect hangs up early, the telecomputer isn't bothered. Telecomputers can take all the phone abuse in the world and go on to dial the next number.

Telecomputers can reduce the turnover in the sales force too. If a salesperson is expected to set up three face-to-face appointments a day to sell a product or service, this may require fifty cold phone calls a day. He or she must brace for an average of 250 rejections each week, 50 weeks a year. The pressure can become intense if the compensation program is straight commission. Few people have the ability to thrive under this type of emotional arrangement.

Rather than have a sales force spend valuable time, money, and energy canvassing or making cold calls, it's being done by computer dialers. Telecomputers have the ability to dial hundreds of prospects a day, hold two-way conversations, and deliver only these qualified prospects interested in doing business.

Sears, Roebuck and Company uses telecomputers to notify customers when their catalog orders are ready. Political candidates use them to canvass voters. Schools use them to check on truant students.

Retailing for between $3000 and $10,000, these automatic callers and recorders can complete more than a call a minute. Depending on the model, telecomputers can place between 512 and 7160 total calls without a human attendant.

ACTIVATING PROSPECTS BY TELEPHONE

Visualon is a company that has learned a variety of telephone prospecting lessons. The name of their game is finding qualified prospects. Once found, their activation rate is high.

In general, Cleveland-based Visualon finds that they can activate a qualified prospect on the first call. At other times, a catalog brochure, or sample mailing is required, followed by a second phone call.

In Visualon's top market segments, 35 percent of the list names are qualified. More than 50 percent of these qualified names are sold by phone. Telephone orders range from $50 to $1500 on five to six completed calls per hour.

Originally, Visualon's prospecting program unearthed qualified prospects for field representatives. However, enough accounts were activated and sold by phone that expansion into new markets was achieved without increasing the size of their sales force. Consequently, field representatives now personally handle only the largest and most complex accounts.

Visualon's telemarketing activation program provides several advantages:

- Rapid market analysis
- Easily refined scripts
- Quickly evaluated list segments

Visualon determined that schools, hospitals, and manufacturing firms represented its best prospects. The phone program helps reach a wider range of decision makers than is possible through personal sales calls.

Visualon's prospect segment lists are defined by type and size of business. The lists are merged, duplicate names removed, calls placed, and each segment's potential analyzed.

Each of Visualon's business categories is rated for prospect qualification rates, sales rates, and average order sizes. By reviewing the success ratios, large potential market segments are ranked according to their likely contribution to Visualon's profitability. Generally, about 200 phone calls to prospects in a single segment indicate whether the segment is worth pursuing.

Prospecting for New Members

A major political fund-raising effort focused on increasing attendance and membership in an exclusive national organization. Members met regularly in Washington, D.C. for political discussions and domestic and foreign policy briefings. Membership involved making a $1000 contribution.

The prospecting strategy started with a letter of invitation followed by a phone call. Invitations were mailed 4 weeks prior to the meeting. Phone call follow-up was conducted 2 weeks before the meeting.

The phone call incorporated the use of a taped message recorded by a U.S. senator who played an active role in the meeting. A telephone communicator introduced the tape and asked whether the prospect would listen to it. After the prospect had listened to the tape, the communicator came back on the line to answer any questions and take the pledge.

The results of the effort were a success. Of the 17,000 invitations sent, 11,786 of the prospects were reached by telephone and given the opportunity to join. Those who agreed to join numbered 219, while 728 agreed to contribute but not join. The total dollars pledged were $329,611, averaging $348.05 per pledge. The cost of the program was only $55,000. After the meeting was over, approximately $175,000 was collected and the follow-up on the outstanding pledges was stopped.

Telephone Follow-Up

Louisiana National Bank (LNB) used an outbound telemarketing program to activate customers who did not respond to their direct-mail campaign. The phone call focused the prospect's attention on the bank's offer. The benefits and features of LNB's bill system were presented in a personalized telephone sales message. Responses to a wide range of questions that might hold the customer back from accepting the offer were prepared for the telephone sales representatives.

Louisiana National Bank's telephone program zeroed in on customers with a moderate interest level and made an offer in a most convincing and personal way.

The bank's telephone operators played a personal message to phone respondents recorded by its bank president. This technique was successful because it served as a door opener and demonstrated the commitment of Louisiana National Bank to the innovative service.

Activating accounts by telephone in the banking industry is important for two reasons:

1. The cost per new account is generally less than those obtained through other media.

2. Efficient cross-selling programs generate new income-contributing accounts that might not be brought in by other means.

In Louisiana National Bank's case, 35 percent of those contacted by phone agreed to join.

UPGRADING PROSPECTS BY TELEPHONE

The key to upgrading a prospective customer to a new level of activity is knowing what action you want the prospect to take: attend a demonstration, ask for more information, ask for a sales call, or make a new buying decision.

The telephone is one of the best back-end tools to improve the cost-to-sales ratio. Calling the prospect back and asking questions will determine if a real interest exists. After identification of qualified prospects for upgrading, the sale can be completed over the phone or salespeople can be sent out on calls.

The telephone upgrading process consists of the following five steps:

1. Opening the conversation by locating the appropriate prospect
2. Qualifying the prospect to determine the level of interest
3. Presenting the message to the interested party
4. Closing the sale by obtaining an agreement to the purchase
5. Servicing the account by isolating other needs to meet and problems to solve

This strategy has another benefit. The better qualified the prospect, the higher the sales conversion rate. More sales then helps motivate the entire sales force.

Telephone upgrading also helps nonbuyers begin to think in terms of upgrading the next time they buy.

Upgrading Periodic Donors

A religious organization was interested in upgrading periodic donors to monthly support partners. They established a telephone program to challenge and upgrade their donors' level of involvement. Wishing to instill in the donors a real sense of belonging, the organization implemented a highly personalized pledge-partner program.

Once scripts were written and phone numbers obtained, calling through the list began. Of the 3406 periodic donors contacted, 23 percent of them pledged to support the organization each month, with a total monthly pledge amount of $9645.

The total dollars pledged over the 12-month period, including one-time gifts, was $122,789. The cost of the upgrading program was $9945 resulting in a cost-to-revenue-pledged ratio of just over 8 cents. Since the monthly giving partners in this organization account for 94 percent of the monies pledged, the upgrade program also expanded the core group's giving base.

REACTIVATING PROSPECTS BY TELEPHONE

Cable TV Subscribers

The telephone is playing an increasingly important role in the cable TV industry. Although door-to-door prospecting is still their primary marketing tool, the decision of when to use door-to-door versus the telephone varies from market to market. Joyce Cable, which operates systems in Wisconsin and Illinois, uses door-to-door to reach people who have not responded to other forms of marketing.

However, Joyce Cable has found the telephone to be the most effective method in customer-recovery programs. Telemarketing also creates leads for their door-to-door representatives. In the cable industry, the phone seems to work best in suburban and metropolitan areas. Poor response to the phone occurs in rural areas. Cable TV also uses phones successfully to launch new products and promotional campaigns.

Membership Drives

As part of their membership drives, associations have successfully leveraged people whose memberships have expired. The National Rifle Association (NRA) is a fraternity of firearms owners, hunters, target shooters, and collectors. The NRA achieved a new landmark in its 110-year history in 1981. Their membership surpassed 2 million active participants, a doubling of NRA's size and strength in just 3 years. This growth brought the NRA out of a $2.4 million deficit in 1979 into a profit position in 1981.

The NRA's membership growth strategy in 1979 involved leveraging its current members to bring in new members. The second plank of the plan was to reactivate its large file of lapsed memberships.

The NRA mailed quarterly prospect packages to the active members asking them to recruit new members. Their reward for bringing in new members varied from hats to license-plate frames, belt buckles, special membership status, and even a four-wheel drive vehicle.

Mailings and phone calls were made to previous members to reintroduce them to the National Rifle Association. The large file of former NRA members became one of the NRA's best new-member prospecting files.

A weak renewal program caused the NRA to pay careful attention to what was needed in their renewal efforts. Now the NRA mails six notices and follows with a phone call to get a current member to reactivate. The first renewal notice is mailed 3 months prior to the expiration date. The NRA waits a month. If renewal has not occurred, then mailings continue monthly through the cycle. The final attempt to reactivate a member whose membership has expired is through a telephone call.

SUMMARY

Getting the prospective customer to take the first step is the secret to successful prospecting. Once the prospect decides to take the initiative, the salesperson can focus on closing the sale. Salespeople often rush out with a low percentage of qualified leads. Instead, they should spend more time thinking, researching, preparing, and testing campaigns and techniques that get prospective customers to respond.

Perhaps the most productive technique in today's prospecting environment is to appeal to the prospects' impulses by providing them with instant accessibility. This is achieved through a telephone WATS line. A small number of incoming Wide Area Telecommunications Service (WATS) lines can be attended by trained telemarketing sales representatives. When prospects call for information about a product or service, the representative determines the extent of the interest and whether or not a salesperson should call on the new prospect. If so, information about the prospect is passed on to the sales office.

Telephone prospecting techniques should provide valuable information to help solve the following challenges:

- How to canvass for prospects
- How to approach prospects
- How to get in to see prospects
- How to survey the needs of prospects
- How to sell to prospects
- How to answer objections and handle resistances of prospects
- How to ask prospects for the order
- How to bring the sale to a close
- How to service prospects after they become clients

Selling

Do you know who the Fuller Brush man of the Information Age is? It is the telephone sales representative. Welcome to the world of high-productivity telemarketing—the latest ingredient in the corporate mix: smoked glass booths, plush carpeting, and a paperless computerized operation. Instead of selling hairbrushes door-to-door, the Fuller Brush man in the Information Age punches in telephone numbers, reaches prospects and markets—doing anything from collecting research data to closing a sale.

Telemarketing is the systematic use of telephone contact for sales and marketing functions. It's using the telephone to increase sales effectiveness while reducing costs.

Sales by telemarketing passed $100 billion in 1984 and are forecast to reach $160 billion by 1986. Some estimates project 8 million new jobs in telemarketing by the year 2000.

BOOSTING SALES BY TELEPHONE

Forward-thinking business owners build on three rhyming words as the foundation for boosting the sales of their products and services: goal, role, and toll. Telemarketing sales programs require carefully designed goals, clearly defined roles, and a task-oriented toll as benchmarks for success.

Setting Goals

To boost your company's sales through telemarketing you must first set goals. (See Table 2.) In a recent election, the goal of a major donor program was to increase pledge amounts from campaign contributions. A taped message from a U.S. senator in the telephone presentation improved the credibility of the campaign, resulting in a significant increase in giving levels.

The recorded message ran about 120 seconds, stressing the reasons for his candidacy and making a specific request for financial assistance. The telephone sales representative introduced the tape and came back on the line after the tape was played to ask people to make a pledge.

A comparison of the phone call based on the communicator's presentation alone versus a phone call incorporating a taped message provided some intriguing results. The inclusion of the taped message boosted sales dollars per hour by 30 percent. The dollars pledged by donors not hearing the tape were only $117 per hour, while the dollars pledged by the supporters hearing the senator's taped message were $152 per hour. In other words, for every hour spent on the phone program, an additional $35 was pledged with the addition of the taped message.

Product marketers have taken a careful look at Grollier's powerful encyclopedia telemarketing sales effort. In 1978, Grollier set a goal to sell encyclopedias by phone. Two years later the telephone sales of encyclopedias surpassed the door-to-door operation. Grollier's boost in sales of 1.5 million encyclopedias translated into a $40 million revenue increase.

Defining Roles

The second building block of successful telemarketing sales programs is clearly defined roles, such as job descriptions and reporting structures.

Some companies incorporate formal telemarketing roles, while others more or less evolve into roles as did Amekor Industries of Pennsylvania. Today, six Amekor salespeople ring up $110,000 in wig sales on a phone

TABLE 2 Telephone Marketing Goals*

	Customers		Prospects	
	Current	Expired	Inquiry	Select
A. OUTBOUND				
1. CLOSE				
a. Sell				
(1) Reactivation (expires)		x		
(2) New customers				x
(3) Follow-up and convert			x	
(4) Marginal accounts	x			x
(5) Follow-up mail	x	x	x	x
b. Take an order				
(1) Continuity (keep out competition)	x			
c. Upgrade				
(1) New products and/or services	x			
(2) Current mail orders	x			
2. LEADS				
a. Generate	x	x		x
(1) Appointments				
(2) Referrals				
(3) Branch traffic				
b. Screen and qualify			x	
c. Follow-up and reactivate		x	x	
3. GATHER INFORMATION				
a. Survey	x	x	x	x
(1) Primary call thrust				
(2) Secondary call thrust				
b. Research	x	x	x	x
4. PROVIDE INFORMATION	x	x	x	x
a. Primary call thrust				
b. Secondary call thrust				
5. IMPROVE CASH FLOW	x	x	x	x
a. Front end				
(1) Credit check				
(2) Ask for credit card/P.O.				
b. Back end				
(1) Confirm				
(2) Collect				
6. SERVICE	x	x	x	x
a. All the above plus *immediate* response to problems				
B. INBOUND				
1. CLOSE				x
a. Sell: Convert inquiries to orders				
b. Take an order	x			
(1) Upgrade from one level to another				
(2) Add-on volume (price incentive)				
(3) Cross-sell related items				
(4) Up-sell specials				
2. LEADS-INQUIRIES			x	
a. Capture names				
b. Screen				
c. Qualify				
d. Appointments				
3. GATHER INFORMATION	x	x	x	x
a. Call patterns				
b. Revenue related (orders/inquiries)				
c. Administrative related				
(1) Shipping				
(2) Billing				
(3) Product problems				

*Adapted from "How to Successfully Market Bank/Financial Services by Telemarketing," a workshop co-chaired by Rudy H. Oetting and Geri Gantman.

bill of $3300. It wasn't always so easy for Amekor, which now manages more than 800 long-term accounts.

In 1966 an aggressive salesman landed in Richmond, Virginia with Bony cuts, fluffs, shags, pages, and perms. One buyer after another canceled or postponed the appointments. Frustrated and tired, the salesman canceled his last appointment and talked to the buyer on the phone instead. The call resulted in the only sale of the trip—a $3000 order for the hair goods.

When the salesman returned home, he called the other buyers who had refused to see him. He generated orders from five out of six of them—all by phone. During the next 6 years, this technique was perfected and the corporate role for telemarketing sales for Amekor evolved.

When new technologies made traditional wigs obsolete and many poor-quality imitations created public suspicion of the product, half the country's hair goods companies closed their doors. Yet low telephone sales expenses and clearly defined telemarketing roles saw Amekor through the distress. With profit margins at about 30 percent, Amekor was able to boost sales to over $1.5 million in 1982. Amekor's six salespeople rarely venture outside the Pennsylvania headquarters.

To outflank your competitors, start by defining the role of telemarketing in the marketing mix. Today's high cost of expanding a sales program based on direct selling may force you to seek the market segmentation and testing potential of telemarketing.

A telemarketing program allowed a small company to gain ground on entrenched competitors and product groups. A 2-month testing phase began with their current customers and then expanded to other market segments. Outside lists, defined by type and size of business, provided a new source of leads.

After a sampling of 200 calls to any one segment, the viability of new prospects was rated according to the prospect's qualifications, sales, and average order size. By reviewing these success ratios, market segments could be analyzed in terms of profitability potential and return on investment.

Next they determined the optimum call frequency for different customers based on size and timing of orders, account complexity, and competitive pressure. Separately maintained from the outbound telephone operation was a toll-free 800 number for customer reorders and questions.

To complement their telemarketing efforts, advertising and direct-mail promotions were continued, providing an important source of leads. Eight telemarketing operators work 4-hour shifts—two for incoming calls and six for outbound calls. Working 4-hour shifts keeps operators fresh and prevents "burn out."

Weighing the Toll

The third building block for business owners is the toll—the required resources to establish a telemarketing sales center. (See Table 3.)

Nowhere are the corporate sales-boosting efforts better symbolized or executed than at the Bell System Sales Center in Kansas City, Missouri. This telemarketing center successfully uses telemarketing to sell telemarketing.

The center has grown from 33,000 customer contacts and $8.4 million in revenue in 1977 to 250,000 contacts and $100 million in revenue in 1982 by applying basic telemarketing strategies: selling objectives, development of marketing strategies, testing, measuring results, and retesting.

Fifty telemarketing sales communicators handle in excess of thirty calls a day. Only about 5 percent of the leads are referred to their field representatives.

The in-house data base assists in numerous telemarketing center functions including cost analyses, daily productivity, inventory control, number of contacts, conversions to potential sales, closings, revenue, and cost-to-revenue ratios.

The telephone is boosting corporate sales by augmenting direct-mail campaigns.

- If you offer a direct-mail prospect a standard business reply card plus the option of inquiry via an 800 number, total response from the solicitation is likely to be up to 20 percent greater than if an 800 number is not available.
- Sales from those who inquire by phone are likely to be as much as four times greater in frequency than those who inquire by mail.

Telemarketing Checklist

To boost service and product sales as your telemarketing center grows, establish a telephone selling checklist:

1. What are you trying to accomplish with this telephone call?
2. How can you learn more about the customer's problems and goals?
3. What do you know about the customer's decision criteria?
4. What benefits do your customers seek for their companies?
5. What do you offer that can produce these benefits?
6. What support materials do you have to follow up your call?
7. What are the objections and resistances that customers offer?
8. What are your responses to these objections and resistances?
9. What specific commitment do you want the customer to make?

TABLE 3 Telemarketing Implementation Checklist*

Date Completed		
Projected	Actual	

		A. MANAGEMENT
		  1. Identify implementation team needs
		    (a) Select and notify members
		    (b) Assign responsibilities
		    (c) Agree upon and schedule monitoring
		  2. Determine implementation schedule and milestones
		    (a) Set start-up date
		    (b) Set dates for completion of major segments
		    (c) Complete specific lists showing:
		      • Tasks
		      • Responsibilities
		      • Deadlines
		  3. Complete budget plan
		    (a) Determine total budget needs
		    (b) Determine expenditure timing and cash flow
		B. OPERATIONS
		  1. Obtain required facilities
		    (a) Acquire work space
		    (b) Design space layout
		    (c) Obtain utilities
		    (d) Order furnishings
		  2. Order equipment
		    (a) Telecommunications
		    (b) Data processing
		    (c) Support equipment
		  3. Develop marketing communication plan
		    (a) Segment markets
		    (b) Develop media plan
		    (c) Approve creative brief
		    (d) Develop test plan
		    (e) Complete production
		    (f) Determine distribution-placement
		  4. Complete interface arrangements
		    (a) Establish required interfaces
		    (b) Complete procedures to handle critical interfaces
		  5. Complete call handling plan
		    (a) Establish procedures manual
		    (b) Agree upon informational content and structure
		    (c) Establish method for information distribution
		    (d) Develop reference materials
		    (e) Establish record keeping (data needs and forms)
		C. STAFF
		  1. Approve job descriptions
		    (a) Telemarketing manager
		    (b) Supervisors
		    (c) Specialists and/or operators
		    (d) Support personnel
		  2. Complete recruiting and selection
		    (a) Make position announcements
		    (b) Schedule interviews
		    (c) Set selection criteria and process
		  3. Complete training
		    (a) Agree upon content
		    (b) Complete development
		    (c) Complete delivery
		    (d) Arrange logistics
		  4. Arrange administrative plans
		    (a) Compensation
		    (b) Record keeping
		D. OTHER
		  1. Determine business capacity
		    (a) Production
		    (b) Order processing
		    (c) Fulfillment
		    (d) Finance
		  2. Complete market preparation
		    (a) Target customers
		    (b) Trade
		  3. Prepare internal announcements
		    (a) Notify operating organization
		    (b) Notify staff organization

*Adapted from "Telemarketing Implementation Workshop." Copyright © 1984 by AT&T Communications.

10. What follow-up activities will help you determine if your service or product met the customer's needs?

STRETCHING MARKETING BUDGETS BY TELEPHONE

The best way to stretch marketing budgets and lock out the competition is to improve the customer appeal of your services. The telephone can help build customer loyalty by:

- Augmenting your current services
- Providing client review discussions
- Establishing reviews by customers on your performance
- Updating customer service plans

The value that is built into your customer base is incalculable. There are an unlimited number of ways to meet your clients' needs by phone. The telephone when used to solve customer problems stretches the marketing budgets because a satisfied customer becomes a strong source of referrals. Satisfied customers rarely depart, also saving on customer replacement costs.

New Approaches

In 1983, the cost of an average sales call surpassed $200. This economic pressure brought about a new marketing strategy by many companies. They started replacing salespeople with direct marketing media for low-volume accounts. The field sales force also began to be managed with an attitude of maximum efficiency.

One of the most creative and ambitious examples of using the phone to stretch a marketing budget was tested and implemented by the Ford Motor Company. Ford initiated a telemarketing test program in three cities that led to a nationwide campaign which eventually contacted 20 million households that had automobiles.

Telephone sales representatives were interviewed and hired to work from their homes. They were given a simple telephone script and set to work from their own phones utilizing selected phone book pages.

Once the program rolled out nationwide, a large labor force was mobilized: 15,000 phone sales representatives, 2000 supervisors, and 22 area managers. After 2 years, some 20 million calls produced a total of 340,000 leads. Of these, 187,000 were valid prospects in the market for a car in a 6-month period.

The marketing cost of this program per car sold came to $65. This represents an incremental cost well below that of other promotional programs run by Ford.

Pinpointing Your Market

Another method to stretch your marketing budget is to start by identifying what you are selling and to whom you are selling. A planning matrix can pinpoint where to place your first marketing dollars to bring the largest and quickest return.

A product-market matrix isolates levels of difficulty in the planning of marketing budgets. The planning matrix shown as Figure 2 was designed for a bank to integrate telemarketing into its marketing mix to extend its marketing budget.

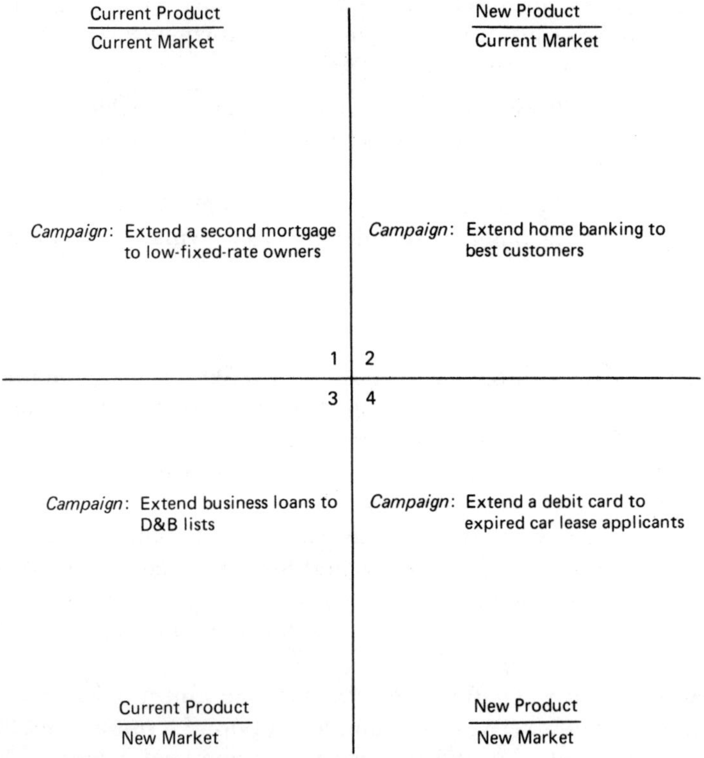

Current Product		New Product
Current Market		Current Market
Campaign: Extend a second mortgage to low-fixed-rate owners		*Campaign*: Extend home banking to best customers
	1 | 2	
	3 | 4	
Campaign: Extend business loans to D&B lists		*Campaign*: Extend a debit card to expired car lease applicants
Current Product		New Product
New Market		New Market

Figure 2. Product-market matrix: levels of difficulty.

Photocopy Sales

Not only have various generic industries capitalized by using the telephone to market their products and services, major corporations such as Xerox have successfully utilized the medium in selling to stretch their marketing budgets.

Xerox Corporation recently publicized their very successful direct-response operation in Henrietta, New York. They sold more than 8000 office copiers outright without having to send a single sales representative into the field to close the deals. This was accomplished through the use of direct mail and an 800 number. The multithousand dollar sales were closed entirely over the telephone.

Telemarketing Design

Designing a telemarketing outbound or inbound "blueprint" will help isolate the interrelationships between departments and personnel functions.

The program should be designed around achieving the major goal of telemarketing: getting through to the right party. Many businesses use screens to avoid telephone sales calls. It helps to know precisely who the decision maker is and the correct pronunciation of his or her name.

However, techniques require testing and refinement. For example, a timely reference to past correspondence with the desired party often gets you through. If all else fails, consider a long-distance, person-to-person call. The long-distance operator will not allow the screen to ask what the call is about but will instead put you through to the requested party.

High-Technology Sweepstakes

Quaker Oats's Cap'n Crunch telemarketing program between July and November of 1981 required extensive planning to execute in a sweepstakes called "Find LaFoote." Quaker Oats integrated an 800 number into the sweepstakes ads, and 24 million kids called for the pirate treasure location. When they called the 800 number, recorded voices told of LaFoote's true location.

Anyone with a map showing the right location was a winner of a Huffy bike, and 5000 bikes were given away. The sweepstakes campaign sold 18 million boxes of cereal, increasing Cap'n Crunch's share of the ready-to-eat cereal market by 30 percent.

The planners, basing their call volume on the initial test, estimated that 10 million calls would be received during the national campaign. However, about 1 million calls a day were attempted, with 400,000 calls per day being completed.

Minimizing Face-to-Face Contact

Telemarketing programs are becoming more attractive because they increase profitability and stretch the marketing budget. Generally, it takes four face-to-face calls to make one sale. This means that the cost of a sale including salaries, commissions, bonuses, and travel and entertainment expenses is approaching $900. The cost is aggravated by related sales costs such as advertising and promotion.

However, adding an 800 number not only increases response 18 to 23 percent over mail response (primarily because it attracts impulse buyers), but it tends to cut down on the number of face-to-face calls needed to close a sale.

Telemarketing Surpasses Direct Mail

In 1981, for the first time, U.S. businesses spent more on telemarketing than they did on direct mail. This represents a major shift in marketing strategies for businesses.

As more and more businesses continue this shift toward an increase in phone use, they need to consider four aspects in the setup of an in-house telemarketing center: personnel, facilities, measurement-controls, and telecommunications equipment.

The main reason businesses are picking up the phone is the rising costs of personal sales calls. The telephone allows companies to stretch their marketing budgets. Yet the costs involved in the setup of a telemarketing center, if not carefully planned and executed, can become more expensive than the status quo.

CUTTING SALES COSTS BY TELEPHONE

> *"Our first and primary service objective is to provide a better and better service to more and more people at lower and lower cost."*
> —*L. S. Shoen, Owner, U-Haul Corporation*

Cost reduction, when viewed as a primary service objective rather than as a reaction to crises, challenges management to provide creative solutions to problems of the marketplace. Cost, in this case, is the cost to business of the values it creates.

In the Information Age, companies are facing a new challenge: to provide more services at less cost using fewer resources. The starting point for cutting costs is measurement. If your costs can be measured, they can be reduced.

In telemarketing programs, the more accurate the data maintained, the better one's ability to analyze a program's cost-effectiveness and profitability. Critical telemarketing data include sales, expenses, and programs.

Sales Analysis

The following is a sample sales analysis and projection tool:

Year	Telemar-keting Budget	Sales Leads	Cost per Lead	No. of Sales	Sales $s	$ Aver. per Sale	Cost per Sale
1986							
1987							
1988							
1989							

Expense Analysis

Sample expenses that require careful monitoring and analysis include:

- Advertising
- Staffing
- Telemarketing operations
- Fulfillment

The following program data also need to be measured:

- Calls placed and received each day
- Call volume by hour, day, and week
- Assigned versus completed cases
- Personnel available by week, month, and year

The 80/20 Rule

How do you determine the best way to cut costs without losing sales? A segmentation technique called the *core group analysis* is a method that determines two things:

1. The top 20 percent of the customers that generate 80 percent of the revenue

2. The marginal and unprofitable accounts that comprise the remaining 20 percent of the revenue

The easiest method for calculating this core group is to arrange customers from highest dollar volume to lowest. The top 20 percent of customers by number generally account for 80 percent of the revenue.

The remaining customers are considered marginal and unprofitable. It is with this group that telemarketing substitutes for face-to-face selling. The drastic increase in the cost of serving marginal customers personally dictated the need for less human involvement in the marketing process by employing direct-response techniques and technologies.

A. B. Dick, a leading manufacturer of duplicating machines, succeeded in cutting sales expenses while increasing the efficiency of their marketing effort.

Sales of supplies to its office machinery customers represents 25 percent of A. B. Dick's total revenue. When selling costs began to rise (see Figure 3), an analysis showed that half of the customers purchasing supplies through the branch offices were ordering less than $200 annually (averaging four orders per year).

The cost of a 1973 sales representative's visit averaged $66 while the average sale totaled $50. The sales call was costing the company money. A. B. Dick realized that their 100,000 marginal customers required a new marketing approach. The preferred customer telemarketing program was developed.

This program included an initial mailing of 150,000 catalogs and a taped telephone script introducing preferred customer service to these marginal accounts. They were reassured that they were still important to A. B. Dick. The program offered a complete marketing package for low-volume accounts. It provided sales information and ordering convenience without a salesperson visiting. Finally, it maintained profitable sales of supplies to a large number of valued customers.

From bicycles to chemicals, industries are turning to the telephone to cut the costs of sales. Raleigh Bicycles uses telecommunications to reduce the high cost of face-to-face selling. In its first year, travel costs dropped by 50 percent. Sales in a single quarter increased 34 percent versus a nationwide decline of 10 percent.

B. F. Goodrich Company used telemarketing to help establish itself as a leader in the chemical industry. Goodrich's telemarketing program reduced the size of its field sales force by 25 percent and cut its sales costs by about $250,000 in 1 year.

Another example of cutting costs is Valvoline's use of telemarketing. Not only do they keep their cost-to-sales ratio in line, but at the same time Valvoline can differentiate its products and improve customer service by telephone. About 90 percent of Valvoline's orders come over the phone and average $10,000.

SUMMARY

Telephone marketing strategies have been utilized to offset the adverse effects of high interest rates, recessions, and sales slumps. There are basically two telemarketing strategies:

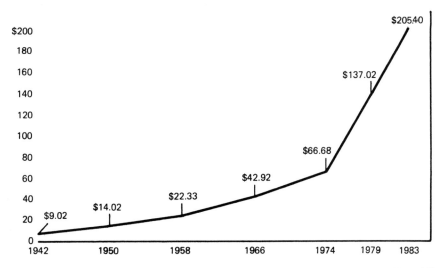

Figure 3. Trends in the cost of an industrial sales call. (Figures per McGraw-Hill Laboratory of Advertising Performance.)

1. An inbound toll-free 800 number to give consumers a vehicle to respond immediately

2. An outbound telemarketing system to increase sales in a measurable way

Before deciding to use telephone marketing in sales one must first consider the needs of customers and potential customers. Then the geographic dispersion of customers and the estimated average order size and potential of each customer must be correlated. Economics and decision criteria then dictate whether personal or telephone contacts should be used. If price and delivery are most important to the customer, the telephone is more effective. If product quality and service reputation are all-important, then face-to-face contact is required.

If only one or two decision makers are involved, the greater the chance to succeed by phone. Next, consider the nature of the purchase. Routine purchases can be handled easily over the phone whereas complex products require direct selling.

If the decision maker is a buyer, purchasing agent, or engineer, the telephone is a cost-effective selling medium. Presidents, vice presidents, and owners expect a personal sales call.

Finally, determine the persuasive content of the communication with the customer. If only the presentation, handling of objections, and the closing are persuasive, perform these steps in person. Then utilize the telephone for prospecting, preapproach, approach, and the postsales follow-up.

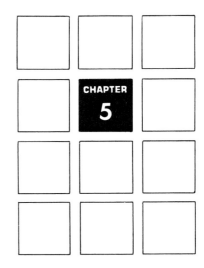

CHAPTER

5

Research

Research in marketing is the "science" of getting people to tell you what they'll really do if you do something. Research was developed as a valid marketing tool in the 1950s, saw its most dynamic growth in the 1960s, experienced a major restructuring of its technologies and techniques in the 1970s, and in the 1980s it is being decentralized as a result of technological breakthroughs.

The effectiveness of research hinges on its ability to contribute to marketing strategies and to provide low-cost decision support. The telephone is proving to be a valuable technology for achieving these goals. It is an accurate and efficient tool for gathering business data and up-to-date statistics. Anywhere an interested party is located, research data can be accessed by telephone.

In the world of research, there are basically three ways to collect research information:

1. *The Mail Interview.* If time is not a problem and a good mailing

list is available, it can be the least expensive research route. Generally a large mailing is required to ensure the proper number of responses.

2. *The Personal Interview.* This is the most expensive method of all. When probing questions are asked face-to-face, people are more likely to give an accurate response.

3. *The Telephone Interview.* The telephone provides accurate data samplings, quick data validation, tight controls on callbacks, an effective medium for interviewer training, and easy interview observation.

Three major social changes are currently affecting these research techniques:

1. *Inaccessibility.* The population is growing less accessible to interviews. First, 55 percent of all adult women are employed full time. Second, the size of the average American household is shrinking. In 1960 the average household consisted of 3.3 persons and by 1990 this will be reduced to 2.4 persons.

2. *Suspicion.* The American people are less willing to be interviewed today. Years ago people participated in research interviews as a novel experience. Now there is less responsiveness and more caution. As a result, the traditional in-house interview is becoming a thing of the past. The telephone is replacing the face-to-face interview as the dominant way to obtain a survey sample.

3. *Technology.* Rapidly developing electronic technology is having a profound effect on data collection. This is permitting better control over the variables and greater accuracy of the data.

The telephone interview was once more expensive than locally conducted surveys. Today a telephone survey tends to be more cost-effective and productive because of its ability to deliver more information in shorter periods of time. Telephone research eliminates marketing expenses and reduces production costs through the speed and accuracy of its sampling.

NEW TELEPHONE TECHNOLOGIES

Teleconferencing

Regional research can be expensive, inconvenient, and time-consuming. In a search for an alternative, teleconferencing was found to provide meaningful qualitative research participation at lower costs than many of the conventional techniques. Teleconferencing saves time and travel expenses. Other benefits include its rapid response time, flexibility, and unique interactive nature. Participants can query the moderator and clarify any misunderstandings that are developing.

Teleconferencing extends the market research capabilities beyond the physical limitations of the in-person focus group. It allows previously hard-to-reach respondents to participate in the comfort of their own homes.

In-person focus groups are often used by large consumer-goods manufacturers for market research. Traditionally they take in only one geographic area at a time. Teleconferencing, on the other hand, can yield a national opinion. The visual anonymity of a teleconference can be advantageous when sensitive or private issues are discussed. Technically speaking, a teleconferencing research project should be conducted by a skilled moderator.

Interactive TV

High-technology television sent over telephone lines is enabling viewers to talk back through their TV sets. Warner Amex's Qube Network, a high-technology cable venture marketed in six U.S. cities, allows viewers to answer TV quiz show questions with a special home console.

The concept didn't take off as expected and network programming was cut back. However, Qube continues to offer breakthroughs in research. A recent project was called "Japan: Touch Now: America." About 350,000 American Qube subscribers and 300 Japanese families simultaneously answered multiple-choice questions about their attitudes on topics ranging from child rearing to handling money. The test isolated key cultural differences between east and west.

900-Number Polling

The use of the 900-number technology is growing by 40 percent each year. The 900 number is proving to be not just a fad but a medium that fulfills the desires of the American people to express themselves.

The beginning of interactive television for the mass market can be traced to October 28, 1980. That night President Jimmy Carter and candidate Ronald Reagan debated. When the ABC network asked its viewers who they thought came out ahead, 469,412 callers picked Ronald Reagan while 227,017 chose Jimmy Carter.

The 900-number poll is very inexpensive to use. Television networks can mount a poll for a flat fee of $25 (with a 500-call minimum). The 50-cent call is charged to the participant's home phone. Billing is done by the phone company, and the revenue goes straight into its coffers. The Carter-Reagan poll grossed $348,214 for Ma Bell.

NEW TELEPHONE TECHNIQUES

Verbose Pollster

Most opinion researchers seek precise answers to fit into a multiple-choice questionnaire. However, the interviewers for the Quester unit of Communication Development Company encourage verbosity. Their phone conversations typically last 20 minutes or more.

Here's how it works: The respondents' words are transcribed in toto overnight by a dozen typists and fed into a computer that sifts out frequently recurring words. Researchers then analyze their significance in context.

The Quester method begins with interviewers asking open-ended questions, trying to get people to develop a train of thought on a subject. This is difficult when half of the people refuse to talk at all. Then another segment talks on at length about subjects unrelated to the question.

The transcribed interviews are fed into the computer, which can recognize 16,000 words. The computer ranks each word by frequency of usage, and researchers review the printouts of sentences containing the key words. Quester conducts 100 to 1300 extensive interviews per survey, accumulating a huge volume of verbiage. Along with the data comes a set of recommendations by Quester.

Telephone Polling

Network and cable television shows are beginning to utilize the 900-number technique for involving the viewers as participants. Dick Clark Productions reported 1 million 900-number calls in 10 weeks of *American Bandstand.* Recently a 900-number poll was used to judge the results of the "most beautiful girl in the world" beauty contest.

On ABC's *Nightline,* viewers were polled on subjects ranging from the Grenada invasion to whether the United Nations headquarters should stay in this country. ABC News vice president George Watson defends the accuracy of the 900-number polling technique. "My recollection is that in recent memory, three out of four of the [*Nightline* 900 polls] results have been identical to the formal poll."

Audience polling is a popular pastime for late night entertainment. MTV's *Friday Night Video Fights* is the high-technology nationwide version of the local "battle of the bands" contests of the 1960s. Viewers vote by phone for the best rock and roll video. NBC's *Saturday Night Live* used a 900-number poll to get audience reaction to the off-beat humor of comedian Andy Kaufman. The nationwide audience voted Kaufman off the show forever.

Communications Audit

The cable TV industry is utilizing telephone communications audits as a tool for determining its community image. Because cable systems offer basically a local service, it is important that residents perceive the cable companies as local businesses. Any damage to a company's reputation can be picked up through the communications audit.

A communications audit is a series of questions designed to measure public perception of the system. The audit report recommends ways to favorably change the community's perception of the company. The cable system then chooses the most effective communications approach for the various segments of the community.

Sales Staff as Researchers

Proper research often results in increased sales. Companies often provide such research for their sales staffs. In other cases, the salespeople must collect their own information. This can be advantageous to the company since the salesperson often gleans more information from consumers than a professional pollster. This information can be obtained from a follow-up service call by phone. When tabulated, such research can often uncover a new market for a product that had not previously been considered.

Subscriber's Audit

The Business Publications Audit of Circulation (BPA) has accepted telecommunications as a means of qualifying publication readership. Publishers can now verify the readership by means of telephone interviews, telegrams, or telex.

If a publisher wants to qualify circulation of a publication by phone, an interview form is developed. Specific interview questions are approved by the BPA before the audit can be used. The interviewer then must tape record the phone calls (and inform the interviewee of the fact) so that the BPA auditors can check on their validity.

TELEPHONE RESEARCH APPLICATIONS

The design of market research projects follows a basic format:

I. Establish the research objective
II. Select a survey method
   A. Personal interview

      B. Telephone interview
      C. Mail survey
      D. A combination of the above
  III. Determine sample size and makeup
  IV. Prepare and test the survey
   V. Execute the survey
  VI. Process the responses
 VII. Analyze the information
VIII. Prepare a report of the findings

Market research projects can be lumped into six categories:

1. *Advertising.* Includes concept, copy, media, and motivation
2. *Business.* Includes acquisition and diversification analysis, trend and forecasting studies, and location studies
3. *Distribution.* Includes types, performances, and channels
4. *Price.* Includes pricing options, profit potential, pricing by market segment and geographic area
5. *Product.* Includes R&D, product enhancements and acceptance, competitive analysis, and testing and packaging studies
6. *Sales.* Includes market potentials, market share studies, demographic analysis, sales trends, and attitude and motivational studies

The following are examples of how the telephone is becoming an integral part of applications research:

Opinion Polling. The 900 number is a popular incoming polling tool for the masses. Its uses vary from opinions on the designated hitter rule in baseball to a guilty or innocent verdict on a TV mystery thriller. The outgoing polling tool of the WATS phone line eliminates all geographic limitations of face-to-face interviewing.

Values-Lifestyles-Psychographics. Many companies are turning to the telephone to reduce the costs of focus group research and to determine the deeper issues of research. It is a communications medium that can provide personalized feedback on detailed research surveys.

Segmentation Analysis. Computers can provide the multivariable analyses that profile the targeted consumers. Touch-tone phones can provide the response mechanism to isolate the needs and wants of the consumers. Preprogrammed interviews can be carried out by telecomputers. Answers are punched in by the respondent through a Touch-tone phone.

Retail Audits. Researchers can perform sales audits of specific brands within various product groups and key them into a hand-held computer.

When the portable computer is hooked up to a modem, the information can be phoned back to a central computer. The market status of specific brands can then be instantly determined.

Consumer Panels. The information from demographically representative households can be reported over the phone continually without the need for a research interviewer. The participants can punch in coded numbers from a catalog to a central computer to report on their product usage.

Day-After Calling. Researchers can call a given sample of the population the day after a television program was aired and ask if the respondents remember the advertisements. The WATS line facilitates this process.

Mail Survey. Rather than have respondents return a written survey, invite them to call a toll-free number and punch their answers into a computer through their Touch-tone phone, 24 hours a day.

SUMMARY

Today's marketing research can be likened to a science fiction movie: American buyers are being monitored by laser scanners, lie detectors, brain-wave readers, computer analyses, and other sophisticated techniques. Computers hooked up with telephones can randomly select phone numbers. The computer dials the phone and places the call from a preprogrammed polling audio tape. Answers are punched into computers through the respondent's Touch-tone phone. The data is electronically gathered and sorted over telephone lines. Computers produce an array of useful marketing reports.

The new data-collection technology is making it possible to produce entirely new kinds of research information and to repackage previously collected research data. The telephone-computer synergism is making it possible to gather, compute, and generate large masses of data.

As the costs of the technologies are reduced and the research techniques become "user friendly," the exclusive hold by researchers over the research tools and data is being eliminated. Marketing managers are gaining more direct access to research information and becoming more adept at using it. This is pressuring the researchers to move beyond simply reporting on market status or advertising effectiveness. They are now using the technologies to produce scenarios and models to project the outcomes of alternative marketing programs.

Because of the new technology, the role of marketing research is becoming more integrated into the flow of the marketing activities. Research can now generate new options from within a company's current market structure. The challenge for business executives is to know what information they are seeking before they sort through the volumes of research data. With the pace of change in our society, seeing the big picture of research is more important than ever. Research data is not informational until it has been processed through a marketing information matrix that determines the corporate research needs. A marketing matrix addresses basic product and service issues such as:

- Who is the customer?
- What problem does the product or service help solve?
- How does the product or service benefit the customer?
- Why does the customer buy the product or service?
- What are the important features of the product or service to the customer?

With the social and economic shifts in our society, researchers are testing telephone technologies that access more data in less time from fewer people costing less money in order to provide better research information.

The telephone is proving to be a fast, accurate, and cost-effective method for gathering research data. The Touch-tone phone, the pre-programmed telecomputer, the toll-free WATS line, and the 900-number line are some of the technologies that will carry research into the next frontier—the Information Age.

CHAPTER
6

Services

The United States has been a service economy for more than 40 years. The transformation of the economy from goods-producing to service-based occurred as a result of four major shifts:

1. The displacement of goods by services at the cutting edge of economic growth
2. The growth of the not-for-profit and government sectors
3. The increasing value of human labor
4. The internationalization of the business system

Services are defined as all output that does not come from the four goods-producing sectors: agriculture, mining, manufacturing, and construction. The four service sectors are as follows:

- *Distributor.* Wholesale and retail trade, communications, public utilities, etc.
- *Producer.* Accounting, legal, marketing, banking, architectural, engineering, consulting, etc.

- *Consumer.*   Restaurants, hotels, laundries, etc.
- *Nonprofit Sector* and *Government.*   Education, health, national defense, justice, etc.

Services dominate the U.S. economic structure:

- Two-thirds of our gross national product originates in services.
- Seventy-four percent of all American workers are employed in the service sector.
- Of the 19 million new jobs created in the 1970s, 89 percent were service-oriented.
- In 1981 Americans spent nearly four times more on services ($880 billion) than on durable goods ($230 billion).
- The United States maintains 20 percent of the $350 billion world services market.

The service industry is extremely diverse. Its very size has dampened the impact of recessions in the manufacturing sector. During the recession of 1974–1975, consumer spending for durable goods dropped by nearly 8 percent while personal spending for services grew by more than 2 percent. The service industry absorbed millions of factory workers displaced by technology and declines in productivity. It has provided more new jobs to women, minorities, and the baby-boom generation than any of the other economic sectors.

The world will never outgrow its need for services. Telephone technology is meeting this demand for the growth of services. To draw a parallel, when the automobile was invented its main purpose was to pull wagons. Years later it actually helped create suburbia. When the telephone was invented in 1876, it allowed people to communicate in a new way. Today the telephone is creating a global economy through instant communications.

Anyone in the service industry needs to recognize three critical issues to enhance service effectiveness:

1. The importance of the service sector in the national economy
2. The importance of the telephone in the service sector
3. The choice for service growth—automate or evaporate

This chapter illustrates the corporate and entrepreneurial efforts to integrate telephone technology into their services.

FINANCIAL SERVICES BY TELEPHONE

Home Banking

A technological breakthrough in the banking industry is dramatically altering the delivery of financial services. The 1950s were marked by the invention of magnetic character recognition systems. The 1960s saw the development of credit cards and automated teller machines. The 1970s brought debit cards, point-of-sale transactions, and personal computers. In the 1980s we are seeing the advent of home-delivery systems and nationwide networks.

As home banking emerges, it is creating a universal payment system. As of April, 1984, seventy-one financial institutions and 15,000 households in the country were involved in pilot home banking or commercial ventures.

Home banking customers can check their balances 24 hours a day, transfer funds from one account to another, keep records on five separate budgets, and pay bills to about 350 companies, ranging from Bloomingdale's to American Express. All this happens from home through a personal computer linked by telephone to the bank's computer.

Chemical Bank recently began advertising its new Pronto System. With a TV set, an Atari 400 home computer, and a modem to connect the terminal via a telephone line to the bank's computers, Pronto does nearly every banking chore except dispense cash. The future success of home banking is directly related to the sales of home computers along with cable television development.

Investing by Phone

As an outgrowth of home banking, experiments are being conducted with home investing—perhaps the ultimate video game for grown-ups. For $17 a month, an E. F. Hutton customer can receive up-to-date information on the stock market and personally tailored research. The execution of buy and sell orders is confirmed over the telephone by brokers. A new venture between Merrill Lynch and IBM could lead to at-home placement of orders. In this case, the system records and stores the client's verbal instructions. A broker recognizing the voice would not have to confirm the order by phone.

Using home computers and telephones to place stock trade orders starts with a few keystrokes. The customer is asked "Buy or sell?" "Number of shares?" "Cash or margin account?" Broker fees vary for this service, but one firm charges an initial $195 fee for the software, a 10- to 40-cent-per-minute connection fee, and the customary brokerage commission.

Japan's Nomura Securities has developed a computer-aided portfolio and investment total analysis (CAPITAL) program. This international investment service allows Nomura clients in Hong Kong and Singapore to conduct business directly with the trading floor via computers and phones.

Targeting a Bigger Market

Charles Schwab and Company, a subsidiary of Bank America and the nation's largest discount broker (1984 revenues: $148 million), is looking beyond the home computer market. Targeting the larger number of clients who don't own personal computers, Schwab is leasing desktop printers and the SchwabLine, a phone hookup to the Schwab data base. This gives clients at 5:00 P.M. what they would get in the following morning's newspaper. The cost is about $45 per month.

Interactive Advisory Service

One of the first interactive news and advisory services in the United States was Electronews, providing subscribers with daily reports on a wide variety of topics such as securities, personal finance, real estate, and taxes. The interactive feature enables subscribers to phone in investment strategy questions and receive answers on their home terminals within a day.

Electronews is now competing against Dow Jones, CompuServe, and Source Telecomputing Systems. Its unique interactive feature and the lower prices (25 percent less than the competition) are helping it maintain a niche in the marketplace.

The system is available in 275 cities. To access it, a subscriber must own a modem and a computer terminal. Subscribers dial local phone numbers and give their special password. The service is broadcast on the GTE Telenet Telmail System for $178 per year.

Telephone Switching

An investor can take several approaches to investing in common stock funds. One is simply to buy an attractive fund and hold it for a period of years. At the other extreme is aggressive "market timing" which involves moving in and out of no-load funds frequently in an effort to profit from short-term market swings. Most investors generally choose something in between. An advisory service like the Telephone Switch helps investors remain invested in stock funds and still avoid most of the price declines.

Several years ago an analyst wrote an investment manual describing a simple, commission-free stock market plan. This was followed by a stock market advisory letter, *Telephone Switch Newsletter*, which uses the plan described in the manual.

Telephone Switch targets investors using the telephone to move between equity and money-market funds within a single no-load "family."

For $117 a year subscribers receive the monthly newsletter, a taped telephone advisory (not toll-free), and special bulletins whenever a switch signal is given. The Telephone Switch is geared to investment in aggressive growth funds that can produce 50 to 75 percent gains in a good year.

U.S. Quotes

U.S. Quotes, Inc., has designed a service that makes stock quotations available to anyone with a push-button telephone. A $45 deposit opens an account. Subscribers are charged 12 cents a minute while the market is open or 6 cents a minute after hours. A subscriber can dial the U.S. Quotes computer and punch in the ticker symbols of more than 15,000 stocks. The computer uses a synthesized voice to give the caller instructions and the latest market information. The charges are deducted from the deposit until the account is exhausted. Clients then make another deposit.

Clients can store a list of stocks and options to keep track of their portfolios without punching in every symbol each time they call. Frequently with discount brokers, customers are put on hold after they request price quotes. Full-service brokers, on the other hand, sometimes pressure customers to make trades. With U.S. Quotes there is no wait and no hassle.

Stock Fone

Stock Fone is also an instant stock quote service that gives data at the push of a button. No special equipment is required and no monthly fees. After the phone number is dialed, the ticker symbols of your stock are entered.

Each time you press one of the push buttons on your phone, you give the computer a signal. The number of times you press each of the buttons is determined by the letter placement on the key. For example, a caller wanting a CBS, Inc. stock quote punches the "2" key three times to identify the letter C, which is in the third position on that key. The user then presses the "2" key twice because the letter B is in the second position. Then the "7" key is pressed three times to indicate the letter S. The numeral sign must be pressed once between punching in the letters. After entering all the letters the stock symbol is completed, and the caller presses the numeral button to hear the latest quote.

A comprehensive listing guide of all stocks and options traded, along with their symbols and full instructions for accessing stocks, options, and indexes, can be obtained by calling 1-800-222-STOCK.

DowPhone

Business news is a call away with DowPhone's updates. Investors and business executives plug into the most comprehensive financial news data base in the world, simply by dialing a local phone number.

The DowPhone data base can be dialed from any phone in the world. It produces audio reports 24 hours a day. The service provides up-to-the-minute business news and information about stocks, bonds, commodity futures, and economic indicators. Subscribers are provided with a directory of more than 8000 codes (7000 of them for companies listed on the New York, American, and Over-the-Counter Stock Exchanges).

Dunsvoice

Dun and Bradstreet's computer voice network is called Dunsvoice. It gives D & B Credit Services customers local phone access to information on 5.3 million U.S. businesses.

The voice network allows 60,000 customers in seventy-nine cities to obtain business and credit information via a push-button telephone. A computer voice responds to customers who request data by pressing the buttons of their telephone.

Business summaries give sales, net worth, number of employees, conditions and trends of the business, names of principal officers, year the business started, and payment habits. Hard copies can also be provided.

Call Prompter

A new telephone feature at the insurance company USAA allows callers to more quickly and accurately route their calls to the service representative who can assist them. The feature is the Call Prompter. Callers are asked by the USAA operator to choose among several options and to respond by pressing a number on their Touch-tone phones. If no option is chosen or if the caller doesn't have a Touch-tone phone, an operator comes back on the line to answer the call.

EDUCATIONAL SERVICES BY TELEPHONE

Registration

Registering for college classes by telephone is now available at Brigham Young University. The system uses a catalog of codes and instructions for using a push-button phone to register. B.Y.U. students use Touch-tone phones to call a computer (which welcomes them), then register, and drop or add classes—at the touch of a button.

Truancy Reduction

The students call it Big Mouth. For parents and principals it sometimes acts like Big Brother. When students at McArthur High School in Hollywood, Florida cut class, it tells their parents.

This computer has an automatic telephone dialer and twenty recorded messages. It reduced the truancy rate to about 5 percent of the student body from 15 percent the year before.

The computer makes calls all day and for 3 hours at night. The machine tells the listener what period the student missed and asks for a note if the absence can be excused. Big Mouth can also be friendly. It delivers messages informing parents when their children have been named to the honor role. In Arlington, Virginia, a Big Mouth delivers the news in three languages: English, Spanish, and Vietnamese.

Homework Hotline

Homework Hotline is aired from 4:30 P.M. to 5:30 P.M., Monday through Thursday, by the Los Angeles Unified School District on station KLCT-TV, channel 58. The hot line targets math and English for junior high school students. This is the time in students' lives when the homework starts to pile up for the first time.

The district allocated $170,000 for the hot line, which drew 3500 calls in its 12-week pilot program. The special telephone number to call is 1-800-LASTUDY, and a teacher answers the students' questions right on TV.

Dial-A-Teacher

Although a growing number of cities are using cable TV for homework assistance, the use of the telephone is still thriving. Brooklyn's Central Library, with funding from the New York City Board of Education, runs a homework telephone hot line Monday through Thursday from 5:00 P.M. to 8:00 P.M. for all twelve grades.

Home Study Courses

Home study training provides no-frills streamlined education. People enroll because of the flexibility, convenience, and low cost. The typical home student is a man (70 percent) about 35 years old with 2 years of college. Women entering the work force now make up a large block of the home study market.

Traditionally, the home student's main contact with the school was by mail. But technology is opening up a new range of options. Many schools have computer delivery of information, videocassettes, discs, videotex, and cable television.

The use of the telephone in home study was introduced by The International Correspondence Schools. A Touch-tone telephone call to a toll-free number is also changing the way tests are taken. Teletest is a system in which students key in identification numbers and test answers. The system replies with the score and tells students which pages require further study.

Telecommunications Courses

Telephone technology is becoming a part of the school curriculum. At Roosevelt University in Chicago, three new courses on telecommunications are being offered as the first part of a telecommunications degree program.

The courses offered are telecommunications (an entry-level course), telephone systems analysis (for further investigation in the field), and C programming language (for advanced students). The courses are designed for students as well as those employed in the telecommunications industry.

Telephone Home Instruction

Computer Curriculum Corporation is turning the Touch-tone phone into a computer terminal with computer-assisted home instruction for children. The subjects covered include math, spelling, and reading.

After receiving a call from the CCC-17 computer and listening to an exercise, students respond using the telephone's own number system. A correct answer elicits an encouraging response such as "excellent work." Children control the pace of the lesson, and the computer adjusts the level of difficulty according to the individual child's performance. The students' progress is recorded and communicated to parents in a monthly report.

Library by Phone

The holdings of the New Orleans Public Library are computerized. The information available in the central library's main catalog is now accessible to everyone from home. New Orleans residents can call up on a screen a list of library books on any subject of interest. If the viewer wants one or more of the titles shown, they may be ordered by phone and picked up at the library the next day.

Electronic University

A former chief executive of Atari, Inc., has opened the "world's first electronic university." Telelearning has instructors for 500 self-paced courses in subjects from art to child care to business management.

Telelearning provides a model for universities that plan to adapt their programs to the new technology. Lessons are conducted between students and instructors via three national computer networks: Tymnet, Telenet, and Uninet.

Telelearning works through a telecommunications package that includes a modem (a device for computer communications by telephone) and software that controls all communications and provides the link to Telelearning's mainframe computers. Telelearning is located in San Francisco.

Satellite Learning

California State University, Chico, has installed a satellite telecommunications link that beams master's-degree classes to Hewlett-Packard Company plants in California and Idaho. Hewlett-Packard's policy is to retrain its employees three times during their careers. The continuing education program using the satellite link is an important step in the reeducation cycle.

Reading by Phone

A unique educational program that aids students to read aloud in a natural and conversational way is offered by Institute of Analytical Reading in Tyler, Texas. Branches of the institute are located in nineteen cities around the country. Instruction can be by telephone or in person. Findings show that instruction by telephone is economical and just as effective as in person.

CONSUMER SERVICES BY TELEPHONE

Horoscopes by Telephone

Jeane Dixon and Arlene Dahl are reading horoscopes over the telephone. Teamed with Productions by Phone, Dahl began her new dial-it service, Lovescopes, by offering advice on love for each sign of the zodiac. Jeane Dixon Horoscope Service recently joined Dial Info in Los Angeles. She also offers personalized advice like "avoid fats." Dixon charges 50 cents for local calls. A push-button phone is required in order to provide your birthdate.

Ordering by Telephone

The field of electronic shopping is being spearheaded by Homeserv and Viewmart, both of Omaha, Nebraska. They bring together retail outlets, banks, and consumers via cable TV. In the future, the conduit may be telephone lines or satellites.

People who use home shopping include retired people who are reluctant to leave their homes for routine banking chores and working people who value the time-saving aspects of the service. The Viewmart home shopping service offers subscribers four ways to shop:

- By retailers
- By services
- By its billboard of bargains
- By special occasion, such as Father's Day

Customers receive program listings for show times and order items over the telephone.

The system provides the opportunity for retailers to enter new markets without the large capital investment involved in establishing new locations.

Instant Gratification

Early Winters of Seattle, Washington sells recreational and outdoor equipment. They offer a program called Instant Gratification in which telephone orders are shipped via express mail. Customers can shop up to 2 days before Christmas, whereas with most other companies, shipments take 2 weeks to 30 days to arrive.

Call-A-Bet

To combat declining attendance while broadening its market, the Meadows Racetrack in Washington, Pennsylvania has pioneered telephone wagering. The Meadows Call-A-Bet system secures the track an average of $50,000 in bets per night. This increases its yearly wagering by an extra $10 to $12 million.

After peaking at $76 million in 1976, wagering at the Meadows slipped to $62 million in 1983. Attendance also fell to 692,000 from 715,000 a year earlier. Call-A-Bet lets customers place bets from their homes through a toll-free number. Subscribers must be residents of Pennsylvania and be at least 18 years of age.

After depositing $50 in a Meadows account, a Call-A-Bet subscriber receives a code name and a plastic identification card imprinted with a four-digit account number and the toll-free phone number. When placing a bet, callers give their account number and code name. The minimum $2 bets are fed into a computer by a Call-A-Bet operator at the track. All calls are tape recorded to avoid errors.

Phone-a-Computer

The newest city meeting places do not serve drinks. They are open day and night. But they are usually so crowded that no one can get in. You cannot reach them by taxi, by subway, or on foot.

These new "meeting places" are part of the bulletin board and message center craze that is sweeping the country. It is an underground obsession for the user and the bulletin board operator. Today several thousand computer bulletin boards exist around the country. They are rather simple to operate and rank in popularity with phoning a friend or mailing a letter. Inexpensive programs let a home computer receive telephone calls and accept written messages.

To operate, users dial up a computer bulletin board via computers. The caller's computer connects to the bulletin board computer. A welcoming message sent from the bulletin board computer appears on the caller's screen. Callers then send typed messages via the telephone line connection directly to the bulletin board computer.

Phone-A-Friend

For those who aren't satisfied with CB radios or computer bulletin boards, New York Telephone is offering a service called Phone-A-Friend. This is a multiperson conversation like the old party line.

Customers in thirty-seven New York telephone exchanges can call one of three numbers for young adults, middle-aged people, or senior citizens. They then find themselves in a conversation with up to four other people.

The first minute of a Phone-A-Friend conversation costs 24 cents during the daytime and less after 9:00 P.M. Additional minutes are 8 cents each.

You don't have to be a talker to enjoy the service. Many just sit back and enjoy listening. Phone-A-Friend employees periodically check on the conversations to see if one of them needs a new participant.

Traffic Updates

In Washington, D.C., WASH-FM's listeners are "on-the-spot" reporters. They call in to update reports on traffic conditions from their car phones during rush hour. WASH gives AM-FM stereos to the participants and pays for their informative calls to the station.

Garden Clinic

From 6:00 P.M. to 9:00 P.M., Monday through Friday, free horticulture advice is given by telephone to hundreds of people who call the Vermont Bean and Seed Company Garden Clinic. An avid horticulturist became involved with the company when she called to place a seed order. The president of the company was so impressed by her knowledge of gardening that he asked her to manage the garden clinic.

Kidsnet

Kidsnet is a computerized system that gives parents information about upcoming TV and radio programs for children. The system is funded by the Ford Foundation and the Corporation for Public Broadcasting. Users can dial an 800 number or tap into a direct computer hookup.

Personal Computer Support

Another twist to consumer counseling services is Personal Touch Computer Advisory Service. This nationwide organization helps consumers select a computer system, then provides hot-line support after they purchase it. Most personal computer owners receive insufficient post-purchase support from retailers and manufacturers. So for a $195 membership fee, subscribers get answers toll-free 24 hours a day.

Turkey Talk-Line

To take the anxiety out of cooking the holiday turkey, a toll-free Turkey Talk-Line is available by dialing 1-800-323-4848 to answer consumer questions from November 2 through December 31. The operating hours are from 9:00 A.M. to 5:00 P.M.

Trained home economists at Swift and Company's Consumer Services Kitchens in Oak Brook, Illinois are prepared to answer all kinds of questions regarding selecting, stuffing, cooking, or serving Swift turkeys. Swift encourages calls from consumers if they are not sure what size turkey to buy, the length of time needed to thaw a bird in the refrigerator, or how to cook a turkey in the microwave oven.

Preserve-a-Pet

In 1965 Roy Rogers stuffed his horse Trigger. Since then, pet preservation has caught on. A New Jersey taxidermist is launching a nationwide toll-free "preserve-a-pet" number to handle inquiries from other taxidermists and prospective customers. He will discuss his freeze-dried method, and the pet's final pose that the owner requests.

Dial-a-Store

VIP Consumer Information Service provides information on local companies without inconveniencing store personnel. Participating stores submit the information they want included in the listing such as store hours, location, and prices and selection of merchandise. A 2-minute audio report is produced. Callers tell an operator which businesses they are interested in, and the appropriate tape is played over the phone.

Dial-a-Lie

Do you need a little white lie to get you out of a jam? Relax and get out your checkbook. A Hayward, California woman lies for others for a living. For just $6 you can buy a simple excuse. Something complex and exotic costs more.

Suppose you are in trouble with your boss about missing work, and there is no way you can miss another day. She'll call your boss on the phone and say, "I'm nurse so-and-so from such-and-such hospital. Would you tell (the person who is paying for the lie) that his or her wallet was left at the hospital and to please come get it." Before making a call, she designs a script and reviews it for potential snags.

ENTERTAINMENT BY TELEPHONE

Dial-a-Soap

For many soap opera buffs, missing an episode of *General Hospital* or *Another World* can seem like the end of the world. But for Cleveland, Ohio viewers the updates are as easy as picking up the phone.

By dialing Soap Line, Inc., callers can hear three 4-minute updates of soap operas appearing on the three TV networks, along with advertisements. Advertisers pay an average of $875 for a week of 15-second ads on three telephone lines.

Soap Line has been deluged with calls, at times averaging 4000 per day. Soap Line breaks even with $7500 in monthly revenues. Their initial investment of $20,000 was primarily for the automatic answering machines that can receive 12,000 calls a day.

Dialing for Discs

Hot Rock, Inc. is a 24-hour telemarketing "music store" founded in 1983. It was the first company in the country to offer toll-free convenience shopping for any record album, cassette, or video in print.

Three Harvard classmates have established a business that targets the professional with a credit card: This is a person with little time or desire to shop for records. The secondary market is the isolated suburbanite between the ages of 21 and 25.

With 500 to 600 orders fulfilled daily, Hot Rock has cable's MTV (music television) to thank for its leads. The channel features video performances by popular rock-and-roll groups and is watched by more than 13 million households. Advertising on MTV keeps the Hot Rock toll-free line busy. Hot Rock's long-range plans include broadening into accessory products and movies. With rock and roll comprising 53 percent of the total recording industry sales, diversification should improve Hot Rock's profit picture. They are currently competing head-on with retail record stores, direct marketing organizations, and record clubs.

Dial-a-Story

The Hammond, Indiana Public Library offers a "dial-a-story" service. It is available 24 hours a day and is free to the caller. The library covers the costs which include $900 for the recorder and $20 a month for the phone line.

Game Line

Control Video Corporation of Virginia has developed Game Line, the first home video game library. For $59, subscribers purchase control boxes resembling home computers, which link their TV sets to the library's seventy-five games.

Subscribers enter the system by calling a toll-free number and telling the Game Line computer which game they want to play. Each call costs $1 and provides ten to twelve "plays" which can last 40 minutes.

Dial-a-Trivia, Joke, Gossip

In Baltimore, callers can settle their Trivial Pursuit arguments by dialing the Trivial Pursuit Line. If they want a chuckle, they can call Dial-a-Joke. Or if they don't have enough to talk about, they can dial to hear a gossip columnist.

Pop Concert Guide

British Telecom has launched a pop concert guide to provide up-to-date information to phone callers. The service is known as Pop Ticket Line. It is updated weekly and provides comprehensive information on ticket availability, locations, and dates of pop concerts in the London area.

Judge and Jury by Phone

Phone-in gimmicks are creating interest in some television shows. In January, 1984 on NBC, the winner of a beauty pageant was judged by viewers phoning in votes.

On May 6, 1984, NBC turned viewers' living rooms into the jury box with a bold new adventure in drama and mystery. Inspired by an actual trial, the audience was shown a cheating wife, a loaded gun, and a sudden death. But was it murder? Viewers called the phone number that flashed on the screen and gave their verdicts: guilty, 1-900-720-2200, and not guilty, 1-900-720-2201. There was a 50-cent phone company charge.

The telephone will continue to bring about more changes in entertainment. The next step may be telephone polling that allows viewers to determine the direction of a TV plot. For example, should *Dallas's* J. R. run for president? On *Dynasty* should Crystle Carrington drop husband Blake?

Pay-per-View

Only 7 million of the 40 million cable TV homes are wired for pay-per-view entertainment services. In 1984 pay-per-view generated just $26 million of cable's $7.7 billion in total revenues. But by 1995, pay-per-view could be a $2-billion industry. The only thing holding it back is the technology.

One of pay-per-view's biggest challenges is matching the technology with the way people use the TV. People usually don't plan their viewing in advance, and a lot of the programming is bought on impulse. On the San Diego Padre's opening day of the 1984 baseball season, for instance, some 404,000 phone orders jammed Cox Cable's lines.

Cox is now working on an automatic phone system to solve this problem. Customers will dial a special number, and a computerized voice will instruct them to dial their billing number and then to dial another number corresponding to the event they want to order.

Entertainment Phone Network

The Hotel Entertainment Phone Network gives hotel guests an extension to call for 2 to 3 minutes of information about what's going on around town. Along with the message comes a 20-second commercial. The charge to advertisers is $50 to $60 per 1000 calls. The hotels do not pay for the service nor do they share in the revenues. In New York, the Sheraton Center and the New York Statler are already signed up.

800-LIVE AID

On July 13, 1985, Live Aid Concerts around the world raised a total of $49 million. A major source of revenue was the toll-free telephone line (800-LIVE AID). In the weeks following the concert, many calls were still coming in over the line. In TV fund-raising, this was unprecedented. With most fund-raisers, like the Jerry Lewis Telethon, when the number is pulled off the air the calls trail off. With Live Aid, people just kept calling.

GOVERNMENT BY TELEPHONE

IRS Calling

An IRS computer may dial your home if you are behind on paying your taxes. Internal Revenue Service offices are now using the Automated Collection System (ACS).

The new system integrates computer and telephone technology to control collection accounts. Early returns show a significant improvement in delinquent tax collections. Account representatives contact taxpayers, generate correspondence, and record actions with little paperwork.

The procedure is straightforward. Delinquent taxpayers continue to receive notices from the IRS Service Center, as in the past. If this doesn't resolve the case, it is forwarded to an ACS site where an account representative will make telephone contact with the taxpayer to resolve the delinquency.

The system operates Monday through Friday, 8:00 A.M. to 8:00 P.M., and until noon on Saturdays. Each account representative has a terminal and a telephone that is connected to the call site computer. Cases are sequenced by the computer in priority order, based on such factors as the type of tax owed and the amount.

The computer dials the taxpayer's telephone number, while displaying the account information on the representative's display terminal. The representative discusses the case with the taxpayer without having to refer to stacks of paperwork. If the taxpayer's telephone number is busy, the computer will reschedule the case for another call in 30 minutes. If no answer, the computer reschedules the call for later in the day. When the taxpayer is contacted, the time of day is recorded for use in future contacts with that taxpayer.

Fraud Hot Lines

The Department of Health and Human Services has set up a nationwide toll-free telephone number called the Whistle Blower's Hot Line. It can be reached by calling 1-800-368-5779. Operators in the inspector general's office welcome information about fraud, waste, and abuse in any of the department's 350 programs, including social security, medicare, and medicaid.

Calls at the general accounting office have averaged more than fifty a day since it was set up in 1979. More than 42,000 people have blown the whistle at the GAO by calling 1-800-424-5454.

The President's Phone Habits

Every week, President Reagan chooses a few people to call for a long-distance chat. These people can be community leaders, executives, handicapped people, sports figures, even children. President Reagan relies heavily on the telephone to keep in touch with the views of people outside Washington.

Acts of heroism reported in the press motivate the President to make a phone call. When an unemployed father of eight saved a blind man from being struck by a subway train, the President called. When Mr. Reagan learned that the hero was on his way to a job interview when the incident occurred, he telephoned the prospective employer. The father of eight got the job and Reagan still receives reports from the employer on his progress.

Civitex

Local government officials with a vexing problem on their hands—like a suburban shopping mall cutting into downtown retail trade or a graffiti artist painting up the town—can dial a toll-free number and find out how other communities have tackled the same issues.

Civitex, the data bank of urban projects, is run by the Citizens Forum on Self-Government–National Municipal League, Inc. It can be reached by calling 1-800-223-6004.

The operators at Civitex respond to callers' problems by searching their data base of 2300 cases for similar subjects. The caller receives by mail a one-page project profile, which includes the names and phone numbers of local contacts. The service is free to callers.

Dial-a-Tax

A 24-hour-a-day computer program by Unified Management Corp. estimates 1986 taxes based on 1984 returns and President Reagan's tax proposal. A synthesized voice answers and a name never has to be given. Callers just dial, listen, and respond. This service shows the impact of the President's tax proposals.

BUSINESS SERVICES BY TELEPHONE

Software Support Services

Microcomputer support service is becoming a booming market. A company called InteSol provides technical services over the phone to users of IBM PCs and Apple computers. The Massachusetts firm targets business users with its TechniCall Telephone Support that aids in the use of more than thirty software programs.

IBM recently announced a similar phone-in service for users of its personal computer. Subscribers to the IBM service pay for seven single-topic calls to a toll-free hot line.

The newly formed National Computer Club of Rocky Hill, Connecticut claims it will answer any question about any machine for a 1-year membership of $20 to $30 and the price of the telephone call.

And now Microsoft, the software pioneers, have also established a toll-free phone line for customer questions regarding their software.

Telephone Advice for $2000 per Hour

A California marketing wizard offers his consulting services over the telephone for $2000 per hour. Here is how it works:

1. Callers formulate a brief description of their business and their problem or need.

2. They call the consultant according to a schedule printed in the *Wall Street Journal* ad. He answers the phone personally on the specified days at the specified times.

3. A 5-minute discussion takes place.

4. At the end of the 5 minutes, the marketing wizard and the client both decide whether it is worth continuing. If so, an appointment is set for a 1-hour telephone consultation. The client sends the fee and information on the problems or needs in the interim. If another meeting is not set, the relationship is terminated after 5 minutes.

Women's Business Hot Line

The American Women's Economic Development Corp. (AWED) of New York offers an 800 number for a women's business hot line. The cost for one question is $5, billable to major credit cards. For a 90-minute consultation, the fee is $25. Over the past 2 years, the line has answered over 12,000 questions.

Cityphone

New Yorkers can call Cityphone to locate offbeat items from the vast array of products and services available in the metropolitan area. Cityphone can give information about a pet store that carries roller skates for birds, a novelty shop that sells jumping beans, or a nursery that supplies pebble-free soil for mud-wrestling contests. Cityphone operators rely on everything from telephone books to their personal notebooks full of tips culled from other sources.

Cityphone operators take an average of 200 calls each day between 10:00 A.M. and 6:00 P.M. from a small office in Greenwich Village. The service is free to both callers and businesses that get referrals. It operates to attract advertisers to New York's Neighborhood Yellow Pages phone books.

Tele-Collection

Tele-Collection, Inc. is doing some high-tech follow-up on behalf of cash-strapped municipalities. This corporation is using voice-activated recordings and a computer to bring the voice of police authority into the homes of motorists who ignore parking tickets or fail to buy vehicle stickers.

Tele-Collection netted billings of $175,000 in 1983. The system begins with a phone call made by a human operator, who ensures that the call is going to the right person. If the person agrees to take the call, the recorded voice of a police officer comes on with the message "I'm calling to discuss official business today and will be recording your answers."

The recorded voice then asks the alleged violator if he or she is aware of unpaid tickets. If the person fails to answer, the recorded voice stresses the importance of the question and repeats it. Answers are recorded and transcripts are given to city officials. Tele-Collection then follows the call with a letter to the scofflaw.

Paperless Telemarketing

Telemarketing companies are generating over $100 billion in telemarketing business annually. Yet this is one industry where the ease of entry does not guarantee success. One telemarketing service, Campaign Marketing Group, began in 1979 with six telephones and one client. They found their niche: soliciting money, memberships, and magazine renewals from members of nonprofit organizations and others who donate to them.

To keep up with changes in the marketplace, Campaign Marketing Group integrated the state-of-the-art technology into their operation. They computerized their telecommunications center, eliminating paperwork.

Computers now dial the phone numbers for the operators and display questions for the operators to ask. The operators can use the computer to start a letter on its way to each person called or send a mailgram to a government official. Today Campaign Marketing Group's suburban Washington, D.C., office houses ninety-eight computer stations and a staff of 150 employees.

Dial 976 "Profit"

Telephone numbers with the prefix 976 allow callers to hear short taped programs containing information and entertainment. Dozens of entrepreneurs across the United States are producing a variety of tapes, ranging in topics from sports updates to gay news, and supplying them to telephone companies.

Telephone companies charge anywhere from 10 cents to $2 each for various 976 calls and do the billing. Pacific Bell Telephone Company earns over $250,000 per week from its sixty-two separate numbers. Sundial Productions earned nearly $400,000 in 1983 by supplying nine programs to New Jersey Bell.

A Successful Entry

Careful planning and testing of telemarketing can facilitate the entry of a new product to the market. The telephone was used for the sampling of Barclay cigarettes.

The campaign was launched in 1980. Ads were placed featuring toll-free numbers and offering a free carton of Barclay cigarettes to consumers who called the number. Although the launch cost Brown and Williamson Tobacco Company $150 million, it resulted in a successful cigarette introduction. Barclay captured 3 percent of the market share, which is estimated to be worth $375 million per year.

Security by Phone

Phone companies are looking to a bigger niche in the home security field. Technologically advanced burglar alarm systems are in about 37,000 U.S. homes with a growth rate projected at 60 percent per year.

Calls for help are currently sent out over cable TV lines. Telephone companies, eager for a piece of the action, are looking to install equipment to transmit the alarm signals over phone lines. The phone company's incentive can be seen in the Manitoba Telephone System of Canada. They receive 40 percent of the fee collected monthly by alarm companies.

Voice Response for Pilots

General aviation pilots can access preflight weather information through conventional push-button telephones with an Interim Voice-Response System (IVRS). Weather information is provided primarily by the Federal Aviation Administration (FAA) through about 4500 flight-service stations specialists who handle nearly 18 million requests a year. IVRS, which is an interim system, will operate for 5 years until the full Flight-Service Automation System (FSAS) becomes operational. The service is operational to the pilot community 24 hours a day, 7 days a week.

Telecommuters

U.S. corporations are benefiting in terms of cost and productivity by converting millions of jobs from central offices to remote work sites, including homes. By 1990, the location-independent work will spur growth of a $13 billion market in sales of microcomputers, peripherals, smart telephones, software, and on-line services designed to make such work possible.

In many cases telecommuting improves job performance and productivity and reduces employee absenteeism and turnover. It also provides a wider access to diverse labor pools. The major obstacles to growth of telecommuting are the problems of overcoming traditional managerial resistance to change and selecting the right employees for telecommuting programs.

Realty by Phone

When it comes to realty service, a Phoenix, Arizona salesman has an advantage over his competitors. By installing a cellular telephone and a battery-operated computer in his car, he has instant access to the multiple listing service (MLS). In addition to contacting the MLS from his car, this realtor uses his mobile phone to get information on houses while his clients ride around the city with him.

Limousine Network

A new service, Limousine Transportation Dispatch Network, patterned after the FTD floral wire-service concept, works in conjunction with private limousine operators to dispatch limos to their point of departure. To reserve a limousine anywhere around the country, dial 1-800-PIC-US-UP. To reserve a limousine in New Jersey, call 1-800-PIC-ME-UP.

Interest Rate Hot Line

A company that reports on local mortgage rates has started a telephone hot line that informs home buyers of mortgage rates being offered by more than 100 area lenders. Peek and Associates, which publishes a weekly survey of mortgages, started the special telephone service. The recorded minute-long messages give the average interest rates offered on 30-year and 15-year fixed-rate mortgages and 1-, 3-, and 5-year adjustable-rate mortgages.

The telephone report does not identify any of the 109 lenders in Maryland, Virginia, and the District of Columbia. It urges callers to buy or subscribe to the weekly *Peek Report*. The cost for the detailed information report on mortgage rates is $15 per issue. There is no charge for the telephone service.

Business Pulse

Business Pulse is a new service from the *Los Angeles Times* that gives up-to-the-minute news on late-breaking developments, stock market averages, gold and silver prices, foreign currency rates, Treasury bill rates, current interest rates for money markets, CDs, mortgage rates, prime lending rates, and commodities. Business Pulse gives a 60-second news report 24 hours a day, 7 days a week. The reports are updated every 20 minutes during market hours. Twenty-five cents buys a lot of convenience and information. The service, charged on the caller's monthly phone bill, is not available through coin-operated telephone systems.

Pay-Fone Payroll

Pay-Fone's unique Touch-tone system allows customers to transmit their payroll data over the phone to a nearby Pay-Fone center. Pay-Fone processes and delivers a complete payroll—with payroll checks—overnight. Pay-Fone provides payroll services to over 6000 customers, who are part of a billion-dollar payroll industry.

CULTURAL SERVICES BY TELEPHONE

Art Auctions by Phone

Telephone bidding has altered the course of art auctions since its inception at major sales of impressionist and old-master paintings in the mid-1960s. Over the last decade, bidding by telephone has become increasingly commonplace and a source for much drama. An impressionist painting was purchased for several million dollars by a telephone bid from a car parked in front of Christie's gallery in London.

Anonymity is the main reason that collectors, dealers, and museum collectors bid by telephone. Bidders who are not concerned with maintaining their privacy use telephone bids as a convenience.

Problems cited by bid takers include telephone lines going dead, colleagues tripping over and disconnecting telephone wires, and clients walking away from telephones and not returning.

Whatever the problems, telephone bidding adds substantially to auction-house sales. Total telephone bids at Christie's ten auctions in November, 1983 (the season's busiest month) saw 132 bidders place 330 bids of which 75 were successful, totaling $13.8 million on total sales of $47.5 million.

Telepraisal, Inc.

Telepraisal, Inc. is an art auction pricing company started in 1982. Auction pricing information is entered into a computer data base and made available to the general public by telephone. For $30 or less per inquiry, depending on the amount of information required, Telepraisal provides instant price histories on any of 600,000 works of nearly 50,000 artists.

To use the service, a buyer or seller of art simply dials the firm's 800 number and gives the artist's name and a description of the work to a Telepraisal appraiser. Appraisers call up the price history on a computer screen, relay the information to the customer, and make a judgment about the likely trend of the price. Payment is made by credit card, and, if requested, a written confirmation follows by mail.

The lack of reliable price information led a Roslyn, New York art appraiser to collect regular price reports from thousands of auction houses worldwide and then relay the information to clients by phone.

Telepraisal's clients include dealers, corporations, individuals, collectors, and museums such as Harvard's Fogg Library. It appraised over 4000 paintings in the first year of business.

Dialing-For-Dali

John McKim, Jr., an art broker in Arnold, Maryland, specializes in quality art and original lithographs by Salvador Dali and other world-class artists. McKim provides updates on Dali's status and the availability of authentic Dali art on his Dialing-for-Dali hot line and answering device. This service provides documented information in a constantly changing market.

DIAGNOSTIC SERVICES BY TELEPHONE

Telephone X-rays

Teleradiology has made the specialist accessible. A diagnosis that previously took days is now available in minutes. X-rays from remote medical sites are scanned by TV cameras and digitalized by a computer. These "filmless" x-rays are then sent over telephone lines to a major medical center for analysis. The x-rays are electronically converted to a screen image, and the medical history becomes a printout. During field trials, over 4000 cases were successfully analyzed by this technique.

Telephone Stethoscope

Children with asthma often need to be evaluated by physicians but are not available for direct examination. Four doctors have developed an electronic stethoscope that can be used with the telephone system to assess patients who are not physically present. An electrical transducer replaces the earpieces on the stethoscope. Signals from this microphone are transmitted to a high-gain amplifier, which is coupled by a four-wire connector to telephone lines by a standard modular telephone jack. In tests evaluating lung sounds by a physician present versus diagnosis over the telephone, the physicians agreed in 95 percent of all observations.

Dial Tone

Free hearing screening is now available over the telephone in the Baltimore area. The service is provided 24 hours a day by the Hearing and Speech Clinic at Johns Hopkins Hospital. The screening test takes less than 2 minutes. A recorded voice asks callers to listen for four faint musical tones and instructs them to call their doctor or the Hearing and Speech Clinic if they fail to hear the sounds.

Dial-a-Doc

Orthopedic surgeons and athletic trainers at the University of Indiana School of Medicine make available a hot line to give out general information and refer callers to their nearest sports medicine clinic or specialist. Callers can be classified into three categories: 66 percent ask about chronic injuries, 24 percent require immediate attention for acute injuries, and 10 percent just want general information.

Sports medicine health care for high school and recreational athletes is at a low level. There are not enough professionals to take care of sports injuries. In Indiana, the 24-hour toll-free hot line is 1-800-23-SPORT.

Phone-In Syncope

Telephone monitoring has outdiagnosed the Holter method of monitoring sporadic syncope (fainting) and presyncope events. The telephone is now moving from the university hospitals into private practice to monitor patients.

To evaluate syncope a patient can wear a telephone electrocardiogram (ECG) monitoring system for 30 days. A monitoring device locks in ECG data at the onset of an episode even before the patient reaches the phone, to tap into the system so data can be transmitted.

Pet ECG

An ECG (electrocardiogram) for your pet is now as close as your telephone. Up to 20 percent of all dogs and cats eventually suffer from some form of heart trouble. A group of specialists now provide ECGs by phone for veterinarians to help diagnose animal cardiac ailments. CardioPet, Inc. transmits nearly 8000 ECGs over the phone each month to about 45 percent of the vets in the United States. To use CardioPet, a vet attaches electrodes to the animal's legs, calls the service, and places the receiver in a modem to transmit the ECG.

Shrink Link

Perhaps the only service of its kind in the country, Shrink Link is a telephone counseling service "to reach those who are sick, but not yet seriously, and those who are heading toward being sick but are not yet there."

The fee is $19 for every 10 minutes and is billed to the client's credit card. There is a credit check before counseling. No appointment is necessary. Hours are from 9:00 A.M. to 9:00 P.M., 7 days a week.

People like the opportunity to call anonymously. This lets them get right to the point.

SERVICES FOR THE TELEPHONE

CLASS

Telephone services that let customers know who is calling them, trace obscene phone calls, and reject calls from customers they don't want are being tested in Pennsylvania under the trademark CLASS (Custom Local Area Signal Service). Control of the telephone is being shifted from the caller to the person being called.

You've walked into your house and heard the phone ringing. You rush to pick up the receiver only to find the ringing has stopped. With CLASS you will be able to dial a code into your phone and automatically call back to your last caller.

Another CLASS service is "distinctive ringing." This allows you to decide in advance who you will receive calls from. Preselection of phone numbers will ring your phone differently (such as three quick rings). This identifies calls you especially want to receive.

Under CLASS, customers can initiate an automatic trace of harassing or obscene phone calls. All CLASS services will cost customers about $8 a month.

Paging

Paging services are improving as they are tailored for specific markets. Numeric pagers for business executives, tone pagers for consumers, and alphanumeric terminals for message-delivery companies are now vital pieces of equipment for paging services.

Directory Assistance

Directory assistance has one valuable asset—its data base. The Bell System is testing new ways to sell this computerized data base of names, addresses, and phone numbers. New services being tested include:

- Callers giving operators the telephone number and receiving the name and address of the party with that number
- Callers giving the operator the address and receiving the name and number of the person at that address
- Callers connecting their own computers to phone company computers to obtain listings and bypassing the operator
- Callers getting zip code information or classified ads over the phone
- Callers hearing advertising that accompanies the directory assistance number. For example, a caller requesting the number for Chick and Ruth's Delly could also hear Ruth give a message such as, "We have Kosher hot dogs and hot fudge sundaes. And we are open 24 hours a day."

AT&T in Real Estate

AT&T is in real estate. Their new service offers pictures and information of homes to and from computers or videotex terminals over telephone lines. In New Jersey, 240 real estate agents and customers can view homes instantly without visiting the sites. The service also features electronic mail for instant document correspondence.

AT&T Operator Services

AT&T operators in the future might:

- Call elderly people living alone to check on their health and safety
- Check to see that children of working parents get home from school on time
- Deliver group messages, like party invitations, by phone
- Take messages and wake-up calls

▪ Offer to try an unsuccessful person-to-person call for you later, then call you back when the call goes through

Dial-It Services

The 976 numbers are bringing mass access to specialized information at a reasonable price. The business opportunities of dial-it numbers show a wide range of applications:

▪ Transmitting prerecorded messages, such as cooking tips from food companies
▪ Transmitting live messages, such as space shuttle conversations
▪ Transmitting the live proceedings of distant events, like shareholder meetings

800-Number Answering Services

The growing use of the telephone as a shopping tool has encouraged some firms to establish local, regional, and national networks. They offer the use of their toll-free WATS numbers as a business and marketing tool. These firms provide 24-hour telephone answering services for their 800-number clients. They take phone orders for clients from people who are responding to a television or print ad featuring their 800 number. They charge about $1.25 for every call placed over the network.

Data Transmission Services

Local Bell Telephone Companies are moving into local computer transmission by modifying their existing phone networks. The Bell Companies plan to carry computerized information at bargain rates between computers. "Packets" of data from different computer sources are bunched together, then transmitted over the high-speed line. Bell is setting up to compete directly with GTE's Telenet and MCI Communications.

911 Emergency Service

In 1968 the first 911 emergency system was installed in Haleyville, Alabama to simplify access to emergency help. Though the seven-digit numbers remain in service, the 911 system has cut the response time for emergency service by 4 minutes over seven-digit calls. In 1984 more than 45 percent of the country was serviced by eleven hundred 911 systems. The system provides a comprehensive profile of the caller through an easy-to-read display format. In addition to location description, the operator can specify agency codes and provide information on specific building or residential situations.

Telephone Deletions

The Direct Marketing Association (DMA) is lobbying against some fifty bills in statehouses across the United States that would limit telephone marketing. Telemarketers and the DMA have set out to defeat many of these bills by offering the Telephone Preference Service. Consumers can now write to the association and ask that their names be deleted from national calling lists. The address is 6 E. 43rd St., New York, New York 10017.

Long-Distance Hot Line

A new toll-free hot line is helping consumers choose a long-distance carrier for residential and business services. By dialing 1-800-332-1124, callers are given guidelines on how to select a long-distance carrier. The hot-line service will mail a comparison fact sheet, but won't make specific recommendations on choosing a carrier.

SUMMARY

Service organizations that are developing Information Age strategies need to consider the following: *To enhance market responsiveness requires the integration of the telephone technologies to speed up the flow of information.* Applying this principle to your plans may accrue three benefits:

- Greater service differentiation
- Creation of innovative services
- Improved monitoring that ensures service quality

Technological change is pervading our environment, creating new service opportunities, and improving the standard of living. Successful integration of telephone technology starts with focusing on the changing needs and buying habits of businesses and consumers.

The next step is to identify the technologies that help satisfy these needs by creating new services or differentiating current ones. Finally, success comes through adapting telephone techniques from other services to enhance current offerings.

Marketing services focus on customer satisfaction. In the Information

Age, we will require services that discover, create, arouse, and then satisfy customer needs. Telephone technology is playing a significant role in the ability to capitalize on these growth opportunities.

Products

No longer just an instrument on which to call and talk, today's telephone is part of a complex information network. This new telephone is becoming the cornerstone of a far-reaching communications system for consumers and businesses.

For consumers, telephones are now being equipped with keypads and display windows that show the time of the call and the number of the person being called. They can forward calls to another number and restrict outgoing calls. Phones also offer a variety of emergency features. Fire alert systems link smoke alarms to phones that dial emergency numbers when smoke is detected. A pocket-sized medical transmitter alerts a telephone unit that dials up to two numbers so a person can receive immediate medical attention.

Telephones now monitor room temperature, sound levels, and electrical systems. If a room's temperature rises above or drops below preset levels because of a fire or a blizzard, the device automatically sends a message to one of four emergency numbers. A phone can also be attached to appliances and turn them off when no one is home.

AT&T is perfecting a silicon computer chip that recognizes individual voice patterns. This will allow phones to screen incoming calls. The technology also turns the phone into a house key. A microphone at the door transmits the voice pattern, activating a phone mechanism that unlocks the door.

Linking the telephone to a computer screen generates a flexible information-retrieval system. Viewers can look at an index on a screen and touch it to get more detailed information. In 1946 cartoonist Chester Gould gave Dick Tracy a two-way wrist radio. Except for the long-life battery needed to power it, the technology for the Dick Tracy wristwatch phone is available today.

The telephone is also having a profound impact on the business sector. With the costs of automated technologies dropping significantly, the electronic office is quickly evolving. This technological revolution will affect all companies. Executives, managers, and entrepreneurs need to become familiar with the new systems and technologies: how they work, their method of integration into the office, and the potential benefits of each.

Business communications systems in the Information Age generally pass through five recognizable stages as they are integrated into the corporate picture:

- *Chaos.*   Making sense out of the technology
- *Control.*   Attempting to cope with the technology
- *Quality.*   Technology affecting all corporate functions
- *Efficiency.*   Technology increasing awareness of productivity
- *Value.*   Realizing improved corporate productivity

The productive application of the telephone results from effective communications planning within the context of the overall business plan.

OFFICE TELEPHONE PRODUCTS

In the communications system of a typical business in 1990, digital bit streams will enter and leave buildings, microcomputers will be interfaced with production equipment to remotely control and monitor work flow, typewriters will be converted into communicating word processing systems, copying machines will convert to facsimile devices for electronic mail, and telephones will become digital video teleconferencing systems. Communications technology of the automated office will fall into four categories:

- *Conferencing.* To facilitate human interaction
- *Information Transfer.* To send electronic messages
- *Information Retrieval.* To recall stored data
- *Activity Management and Processing.* To integrate voice and data
at the business workstation

Conferencing

More than 20 million business meetings are held in the United States each day at a cost of more than $250 billion annually. More than 50 percent of the airline tickets sold in the United States are for business trips, while about 50 percent of a typical manager's time is spent in meetings. It has been proved that teleconferencing can save up to 40 percent in travel costs, increase and decentralize communication, and facilitate positive working relationships between users.

It is estimated that every American business has utilized teleconferencing at one time or another. Practically all of these businesses have made a three-way conference call—teleconferencing in its most basic sense. Yet less than 5 percent have used forms of teleconferencing other than audio or audio-graphic conferencing.

Video teleconferencing is the ability of two or more people in different locations to communicate face-to-face across great distances combining both speech and vision, complete with graphics display and the exchange of data and documents. Video teleconferencing makes it easy to hold meetings, seminars, and conferences in which many participants communicate as if they were present at a single location.

A video teleconference is usually held in a permanent video conference room of about 1500 square feet in which lighting, acoustics, seating arrangements, and video equipment and controls facilitate the meeting. A simple point-to-point video teleconference under ideal circumstances could cost as little as $6000. Elaborate point-to-multipoint programs can easily surpass $200,000.

Video teleconferencing can improve communications by making better use of time, money, and human resources. Specific applications of video teleconferencing include:

- New product announcements
- Introduction of new marketing programs
- Motivational programs
- Introduction of new policies or policy changes
- Field support programs
- Sponsorship of educational or informational programs

Information Transfer

On April 16, 1970, the U.S. Post Office Department was reorganized to streamline itself in response to the increasing volume of printed correspondence. But business letters still took 2 or 3 days to reach their destinations. This pace no longer satisfied American businesses. Along came Fred Smith with his "overnight" carrier Federal Express to meet the need. Then the pace of business changed again. The velocity of the marketplace was demanding "instant communication," also known as "do it now." In today's marketplace instant communication occurs in one of four basic ways: direct electronic mail, commercial electronic mail, facsimile mail, and voice mail.

Direct Electronic Mail.   In America, 79 percent of all telephone calls are business calls. While 90 percent of all business calls are never completed on the first try, 80 percent of the business calls completed require a callback anyway. With electronic mail, people can send messages to each other and get requests answered, even though the person isn't in the office. Typically, electronic mail requires a microcomputer, a modem, some communications software, and a phone line to send it through.

Electronic mail is the transmission of messages which would otherwise be sent through the postal service. A significant advantage of electronic mail comes when messages have to cross time zones. You don't have to look at the clock to decide when to contact someone who isn't operating in the same time zone. Electronic mail is also faster and more dependable than postal mail, with the capabilities of hard-copy communications.

Commercial Electronic Mail.   Electronic mail is part of the $8 billion "time-sensitive" mail delivery market. The commercial electronic mail services competing for these dollars include MCI Mail, General Electric's Quick-Com, ADP's Automail, Tymeshare's OnTyme, GTE's Telenet, Comet, ITT's Dialcom, Western Union's EasyLink, CompuServe, and the Source.

By 1989, it is projected that there will be more than 30 million personal computers and tele-terminals installed worldwide. Many will be connected via networks to corporate offices from either field or home offices.

Facsimile Mail.   Facsimile (fax) is an old technology that has been used as a business tool since the 1930s. Facsimile is the most popular form of electronic mail. It produces exact hard-copy duplicates of handwritten and typewritten documents, graphs and charts, photographs, and draw-ings. Fax sends more than 400 million pages a year.

The fax terminal scans the images on the input document and through a modem converts those images to electronic signals called binary digits (bits). These signals are transmitted over telephone lines to a receiving unit which produces an exact copy of the original document.

Voice Mail.   Voice mail is a computer system that communicates with a number of telephone lines, allowing users to record, retrieve, and forward messages recorded with the caller's voice. Also known as voice store and forward, voice mail offers a fourth mode of human commu-nication in addition to face-to-face meetings, telephone calls, and textual mail. Voice mail offers the spontaneity and convenience of a phone call with the time independence of a letter. Advantages of voice mail include:

- Detailed voice messages can be left in the called party's mailbox.
- The office telephone ceases to generate unwelcomed interruptions.
- Voice mail systems can answer incoming calls when the intended party is already talking on the phone.
- Voice mail supports shared usage among many subscribers.

Information Retrieval

Information has four strategic roles in the future of business:

1.   *Transaction Processing.*   Data are made useful in daily business functions.

2.   *Decision Support Activities.*   These are quickly evolving due to software advances.

3.   *Motivation.*   The availability of facts and data encourages the pursuit of strategic goals.

4.   *Competitive Advantage.*   The effective use of technology and information to lower costs, differentiate products, and improve services.

We are moving into an environment where data, text, voice, and images will be freely interchanged between locations via the corporate network. Composite documents of text, data, and graphics with review-ers' comments in the form of voice annotations will be stored and exchanged. In such an environment, compatibility will be a key issue.

Within this complex environment, the telephone industry is bringing out a new generation of phone systems that are able to mix voice and data on the same line without interference.

In order to communicate over the phone system, computers have to transform their digital signals into analog signals—to look like the human voice. A standard modem takes a digital signal and translates it into a warbling sound composed of frequencies in the range of 1050 to 2250 cycles per second—the range of the human voice. At the other end, another modem translates the signal back to a digital form. One out of three office desktop computers in the United States are connected by modems.

Activity Management and Processing

On March 10, 1876, Alexander Graham Bell invented the forerunner to the professional workstation when he spoke words over his first telephone. Today the professional workstation consists of five principal parts: an executive telephone, a data terminal, a speakerphone, a modem, and a step-sculptured keyboard.

By 1988 the market for professional workstations will grow to 8.3 million units valued at $2.4 billion. The workstation typically replaces an executive feature telephone, data terminal, calendar, telephone directory, telephone log, tickler file, scratchpad, speakerphone, and increasingly, the personal computer.

As the velocity of business increases, the professional must rely on up-to-date information for effective decision making. With the professional workstation, access to the most time-sensitive data occurs with a single keystroke.

Features commonly available on integrated voice-data terminals (IVDT) include:

- *Built-In Modem.* Integrates voice and data terminals with other equipment
- *Down-line Loading.* Shares data between host computer and workstation
- *Electronic Mail.* Sends messages electronically
- *Equipment Compatibility.* Critical interfacing between personal computers, printers, external modems, and/or local area networks
- *Hands-Free Dialing.* Initiates and displays call when the other party answers
- *One-Button Log-on.* Allows quick access to over 2000 commercial data bases
- *Programmable Function Keys.* Program frequently used data base access codes
- *Simultaneous Voice and Data Communication.* Allows information to be accessed while talking on the phone
- *Telephone Directory.* Stores and retrieves frequently called phone numbers with a single stroke

PERIPHERAL TELEPHONE PRODUCTS

The following is a partial list of available telephone peripherals. Numerous manufacturers provide the equipment at a wide range of prices. The value of the peripheral products becomes evident as the add-on features help resolve your telephone usage problem without the necessity of completely renovating your current system or installing a new telephone system.

- *Automatic Answering Machine.* Plays and records single-line messages from incoming phone calls
- *Automatic Call Distributor.* Automatically forwards call to the operator who has been idle the longest; gives detailed management information reports; announces "All operators are busy. Please hold until an operator comes on the line."
- *Automatic Computer Record Dialing Machine.* Dials a preprogrammed telephone number, then plays an automatic recording
- *Automatic Dialer.* Stores phone numbers in memory to provide easy access
- *Barge-Out Device.* Announces the outgoing messages to callers
- *Busy-Out Device.* Senses one line that is ringing in, then automatically "busys-out" others
- *Call Diverter.* Diverts calls from one telephone number to another prearranged number
- *Call Management System.* Gives detailed information on telephone calling activities and their related costs
- *Call Parking.* Places a call on hold allowing it to be retrieved from any other phone within the system
- *Call Restriction.* Limits employees to making only certain types of calls, such as internal or long-distance calls
- *Call Sequencer.* Holds calls in queue, answering them with a taped message or music, until the attendant can handle them personally
- *Cordless Phone.* Utilizes FM frequency for transmission
- *Direct-In Line.* Speeds up call handling by allowing callers to reach the people they are calling without going through the central console
- *Intercom Callback.* Provides caller's station number on a digital readout display on the other person's phone
- *Least Call Routing.* Automatically routes all outgoing calls by the least expensive route available
- *One-Ring Dialer.* Automatically dials a predetermined telephone number when the receiver is lifted off the hook

- *Question-and-Answer Machines.* "Talks" to callers, asks questions, waits for responses, and records them
- *Station Message Detail Recording.* Issues a printout that tells who called whom, at what time, how often, for how long, and at what cost
- *Tape Library.* Automatically plays outgoing messages for callers
- *Telephone Record Control.* Records and/or monitors both sides of a telephone conversation
- *Teleprinter.* Produces a hard copy of electronically transmitted data
- *Trunk Queue.* Places an outside call in a queue when no lines are available; caller's phone automatically rings when a line becomes available

TELEPHONE NUMBERS

Companies are starting to use their telephone numbers to advertise, promote, inform, and entertain. They are using inbound and outbound toll-free WATS lines, 900-number information polls, and the 976 dial-it services. These numbers all have one thing in common: They provide instant accessibility to the product, service, or message for millions of callers worldwide.

900 Numbers

When ABC News asked the viewers of their nightly news show to phone in their opinions on the American invasion of Grenada, the results of the unscientific survey backed America's involvement by a margin of 502,358 to 63,812.

The polling technique of the 900 number has increased in usage by 40 percent between 1982 and 1983. The 900 service actually offers two types of calls. One records how many calls are made to a particular number in polls. In this case, the caller is charged 50 cents per call. The other service is similar to local dial-it services by offering live or taped information. The charge for this service is 50 cents for the first minute and 35 cents for each additional minute.

According to the Federal Communications Commission (FCC) in the first full year of operation for 900 numbers in 1981, a total of 10.9 million calls were made. In 1982, 15.8 million calls were made with 6.3 million made to the polling lines and 9.5 million made to the information lines. In 1983, 900 numbers accounted for more than 22 million calls.

The profitability and marketability of the 900 service has made it attractive to AT&T's major long-distance competitor, MCI, which is trying to establish its own 900 service. Since the number was implemented for the Carter-Reagan debate in October, 1980, the polling service has been used by more than 150 companies.

On the information lines, 1,200,000 calls were logged when the National Aeronautics and Space Administration (NASA) set up phone lines for its first space shuttle mission. This allowed the public to listen in on the conversations between the astronauts and mission control. The information service cost NASA $250 a day, provided a minimum of 2000 calls came in.

To sponsor a 900-number poll line, it costs the sponsor just $25 a day for the line with a minimum of 500 calls. The shortfall, in either case, costs the sponsor 25 cents a call.

The United States League of Savings Associations uses a 900 number to provide daily updates on legislative and regulatory news from Washington, D.C. The recordings also furnish quick access to the interest rates established at treasury auctions to financial institutions.

The advantages of the 900 lines are significant. Not only do they save companies money over the traditional toll-free service, but the 900 lines can receive more calls—several thousand calls at the same time.

Evangelist Pat Robertson, *host* of the *700 Club* religious broadcast, sponsored an information 900 number during the network broadcast of *The Day After,* on November 20, 1983. With the show depicting the effects of a nuclear war on a small U.S. town, Robertson purchased commercial airtime to express a message of hope and eternal life. Viewers of the commercial were then invited to call the 900 number if they wanted more information. The 900-number message told listeners of the good news of Jesus Christ. The listeners of the tape were invited to call toll-free to the 700 Club in Virginia Beach, Virginia, to make a decision for Christ or to receive counseling.

Another creative use of the 900 information service number was seen at the U.S. Department of Agriculture's (USDA) 60th Annual Agricultural Outlook Conference. The speeches could be listened to by dialing the appropriate number for the site where the speech was given: Jefferson Auditorium 900-410-JEFF, Forrestal Building Auditorium 900-410-FORR, Room 104A administration building 900-410-104A. The cost for the 900-line service was 50 cents for the first minute and 35 cents for each additional minute. Copies of the Preliminary Outlook '84 program were available by writing to Outlook '84, 900-line USDA/WAOB, Room 5143-S, Washington, D.C. 20250.

To obtain 900-number service information, call 1-800-222-0400. To find out which companies currently use 900 numbers, call 1-900-555-1212.

800 Numbers

Telemarketing has been around for years helping people every day to do more business at less cost. The increase in toll-free numbers has been dramatic. In 1977 there were 80,000 toll-free numbers, while 5 years later 220,000 toll-free numbers were in use. Although AT&T has been spending $13 to $15 million annually to spark telephone marketing growth, the primary reason for its growth is the cost factor.

In a study comparing telemarketing with on-site selling, the face-to-face costs in 1983 averaged nearly $200. And it took an average of five on-site visits to close an industrial sale. On the other hand, depending on the kind of product being sold and the type of client, a phone call can cost between $4 and $40. The three significant applications of the 800 number in business include:

1. *A Total Information Center.* These are established to answer questions from consumers. General Electric's 800 number center handles 4000 calls per day from consumers who want to know more about GE products and how to fix them. Computer terminals provide enough data to answer 500,000 possible questions. The toll-free service costs General Electric $10 million annually to operate. Companies are printing 800 numbers directly on their products, providing a means to answer consumer questions when they arise.

2. *Direct Marketing by Phone.* Telemarketing is a supplement that helps reduce inventories and speed up shipments. The computer keeps tabs on accounts while the phone delivers information and maintains personal contact.

3. *Tracking Advertising.* Companies can place 800 numbers in their ads to track the effectiveness of ads. This also generates an immediate source of leads.

There are several practical considerations involved in setting up a toll-free 800 number. The following list will help you start planning a strategy:

1. *Analyze Costs.* Derive a cost-per-minute figure based on the service by dividing the minutes into the costs. This figure will help you evaluate the sales pitches of common carriers.

2. *Study the Traffic Engineering Tables.* First, look at the service levels and the trunk group size. By adding circuits the probability of an incomplete call is reduced. Second, look at the economy-of-circuit scale.

Bulk purchasing can bring about price breaks that reduce your cost-per-minute figure.

3. *Select Your Vendors.*   It is difficult for a single vendor in today's environment to offer the ideal configuration. Therefore invite carriers to do traffic studies and make recommendations and cost estimates.

4. *Write Up Your Expectations.*   With a WATS line, calling patterns often reflect your business dynamics. Make sure the network matches the demands of the calling patterns of your business activity.

More information on establishing a toll-free WATS line can be obtained by calling 1-800-222-0400.

Many small and medium-sized companies don't want the expense of owning their own 800 numbers. Costs on some 800 numbers can be several thousand dollars per month plus an initial ordering and installation fee.

Common-use services offer the use of their inbound and outbound 800 lines. The costs for these services are significantly less. One company charges its clients a base rate of $115 per month which includes the first 100 calls. Every call after that, up to 500, is charged $1.15. Price breaks over 500 bring the charge down to about $1 per call.

Advertising response rates increase through offering the 800 number in print or TV ads. The common carrier is a good starting place for testing a WATS line and its services are provided 24 hours a day, 7 days a week.

976 Dial-It Numbers

In 1928 the dial-it service started in response to operator complaints at the number of calls for time and temperature. The phone company bypassed the tie-ups caused in the switching stations by installing a line with prerecorded time and temperature messages.

Today scores of entrepreneurs and corporations are establishing prerecorded messages on everything from horoscopes to sports. The calls are produced and aired in cooperation with the phone company. The commissions from these dial-it services range from 10 to 50 percent of the charge. Producers of the 976 dial-it services in New York must guarantee the phone company 100,000 calls a month. Once a month, the phone company sends a report to the producers of the recorded message. The reports are broken down by number of calls each week and show activity hour by hour. The phone company, which does the collecting of the bills, also includes a check.

If 976 dial-it services are viewed as a mass announcement service, it appears that entrepreneurs have brought pay programming and large audiences to the telephone. The mechanism for this business is a type of "leased-access" arrangement. The audio programs range in length from 30 seconds to 3 minutes.

To become a part of the world of phone programming, start by calling your local phone company and inquire as to how you can lease a line for your own business.

Alpha Translations

It would seem that only in America could someone come up with a telephone number and then start a company. This is the kind of ingenuity that started 1-800-FLOWERS. This company now sells millions of dollars' worth of flowers by phone each year. The use of a word as part of a phone number is catching on. To create an alphanumeric for your company, follow these steps:

- Create the word using either part or all of the seven digits.
- Dial the number and see if the number is in use.
- Make sure the exchange and number are available.
- Call the local phone company and ask them to check the availability of the number.
- Place the order and begin to advertise the phone number.

The cost is the same as for your local phone service. To set up a nationwide toll-free WATS line using the anagram, follow the same directions, then call 1-800-222-0400.

TELEPHONE POTPOURRI

Telephone potpourri is a mixture of techniques and technologies which is having a profound impact on the marketing mix. The applications of these product ideas are diverse and durable. This section features interactive voice telemarketing, supportive prerecorded messages, telecomputers, technologies for the handicapped, pay phones, and teletransaction.

Interactive Voice Telemarketing

Interactive voice telecommunication is an inbound direct marketing tool that asks questions, gets responses, and books orders. For greater impact the message to the audience can be conveyed by a celebrity on a prerecorded tape. The persuasion of the human voice combined with the efficiency of the computer makes interactive voice telemarketing a powerful marketing tool.

Interactive voice telecommunication works over conventional telephone lines with regular telephones. The system lets the caller interact with various verbal programs. It creates an informative, interactive conversation in a natural voice, then imparts specific information to the callers.

The totally computerized electronic telemarketing product is the next level in interactive telemarketing. This technology reduces personnel staffing problems and operator burnout. Inbound electronic telemarketing equipment can verbally interact with a telephone caller. The system asks the caller a series of questions directed toward the end result—from taking an order to providing information. The manner is satisfying to both the consumer and the marketer.

The audio storage and dial retrieval system is a computerized method of storing, on tape or disc, a series of prerecorded computerized messages which are automatically located and played for callers. Individual messages are assigned codes which callers access through their Touch-tone phones. These systems provide information 24 hours a day, 7 days a week, from any location to any phone.

New applications for this technology are being created every day because the technology satisfies the need for effective information management. Training, sales support, advertising, public relations, customer service, and general communications are evolving applications for government and businesses in the Information Age.

Supportive Prerecorded Messages

A new approach to telemarketing is the use of prerecorded taped information. Anyone with a tape recorder and a message to give can establish a dial-access program. Advertisements often appear in the classified ads with the words, "Call 224-3399 for a recorded message."

Telephone-accessed informational message systems vary in cost and complexity. Some systems can automatically answer and provide a predesignated message, while others provide access through an operator who gives the caller a choice of topics. The newest models include sophisticated microprocessor-based, voice-synthesized responses interacting with the callers' Touch-tone phone queries.

Companies are making information available for many reasons: to solve a problem for the consumer; provide data on credit policies; educate the consumer on return-of-goods policies, ordering, and purchasing procedures; augment the services to the consumer; introduce new services or products; or instruct a consumer on the proper use or care of a purchased item. Standard labor-intensive marketing functions are prime candidates for prerecorded telemarketing programs.

Telecomputers

Automatic-dialing telecomputers dial a sequence of telephone numbers, without attendance, and play a prerecorded message when the call is answered. Telecomputers play a key role in the selling process because they reach a maximum number of people in the shortest amount of time and with very little investment in human resources. In cases where the key to selling is numbers, nothing beats the telecomputer at this time.

There is a debate raging regarding the use of this technology. Opponents dislike automated dialing of an unqualified series of telephone numbers to procure prospects or sales. They argue that this is in direct violation of a foundational principle of telemarketing—to enhance person-to-person contact.

The beneficial uses of the automatic-dial machines include telenotification and telemessaging to communicate time-sensitive information and other worthwhile announcements: Telecomputers can also dial targeted prospects, but in this case, once the connection is made, a human operator comes on the line.

This technology can be abused. Many people think being called by a machine is a nuisance, and taped messages can be used haphazardly and indiscriminantly for sales solicitations. The telemarketing community frowns on these applications. The use of telecomputers may backfire by tarnishing the reputation of the telemarketing industry.

Technologies for the Handicapped

Telephone technology is creating job opportunities for the 4 million Americans of working age with hearing disabilities. The most popular piece of electronic equipment for the deaf is the portable telecommunications device for the deaf (TDD). This device fits into a briefcase and turns any telephone into a text transmitter and receiver.

Another technological aid is a beeper that communicates through vibrations instead of beeps. A related device changes audible signals, such as telephone bells, into visual ones. The most advanced technology for the deaf is a wireless personal amplification system that converts sound waves into infrared light and then back into louder sound that can be heard through earphones.

Pay Phones

Customer-owned coin-operated telephones are being approved in many states. Residential and business customers are purchasing and installing coin-operated telephones for use inside their businesses and homes. These coin phones must be registered with the FCC or a registered protective coupling arrangement must be used. Phone companies continue to provide the access lines.

Owners of bars, restaurants, hotels, gas stations, and other pay phone "hot spots" are welcoming the change. Bell Companies offer only 2 to 7 percent of a pay phone's $50 to $150 monthly take to the host. The private pay phone companies are giving businesses two options: Lease wall space to a private pay phone operator and get a bigger cut—ranging from 25 to 50 percent—or purchase the phone and keep all the money.

Coin-operated phone owners will be billed for calls that customers make, but will keep all coin deposits. In New York, the initial 5-minute charge for a local call cannot exceed 25 cents. There is also no charge for calling the emergency 911 number, the operator, or directory assistance.

Teletransaction

The automation of field sales order entries requires a combination of software, hardware, and networking technology for an effective, economical information system. This type of program can increase sales, speed up deliveries, and reduce mistakes. A teletransaction system can provide a sales professional with up-to-date, accurate information ranging from customer histories to price changes.

In one company it used to take 10 days for price changes to be implemented in their fourteen locations. With a teletransaction system the price updates are now sent over the network and take effect immediately. Since every 1 percent increase in gross profit yields a 30 percent increase in net profit, the effect of this company's immediate price increase at all locations is significant.

Automated order entry systems can eliminate mail delays, lost orders, write-up errors, data entry errors, out-of-stocks, delayed buyer confirmation, and exceeded credit limits. The two basic options for the automation of field order entry systems are designing your own system or purchasing a vendor's system. When designing your own system, a network of WATS lines links the microcomputers to a host processing computer. Companies using vendor teleprocessing services design the data network as an extension of their in-house data-processing capabilities.

Special Note

The author does not wish to endorse companies that provide telephone products. For this reason the names of vendors have been omitted from this chapter.

SUMMARY

In today's office environment, there is a tendency to misuse the new technologies. Rather than produce less paper, they often generate more. This results in less, not more, productivity. Many elements contribute to office productivity, but none is more important than the effective use of telephone technology. Today there exist so many communications alternatives that failure to plan your telephone use, even for the small company, may be viewed as unsound business practice. The following steps will help you manage the new telephone products and your overall telecommunications system:

   I. Learn about your company's business.
     A. Define your company's key discipline.
     B. Determine the role your telephone system currently plays.
     C. Evaluate management's view toward the telephone system.
     D. Calculate the percentage of sales that is spent on telecommunications.
     E. Map out how management views the role of phones in the future.
  II. Learn about your present telephone system.
     A. Conduct a physical survey and document your present system.
     B. Determine which vendors and services are being used.
     C. Conduct a survey to determine the system's impact on your business.
 III. Learn about your telephone costs.
     A. Review the total monthly and annual costs.
     B. Notice any recurring charges.
     C. Review the usage charges.
     D. Review the installation charges.
     E. Review the costs by department.
     F. Notice the costs by type of service: local, toll, WATS, etc.
     G. Review the costs by vendor.
  IV. Learn your company needs by monitoring telephone system uses.
   V. Evaluate your present telephone system.
     A. Trunking—determine grade of service to achieve optimization.

B. Equipment—observe employees' use of their phones.
C. Services—evaluate quality and cost-effectiveness.
D. Personnel—monitor their performances.
VI. Evaluate alternative equipment and services.
   A. Review costs.
   B. Evaluate levels of service.
   C. Determine ease of integration into present system.
   D. Estimate impact on users.
   E. Review maintenance and repair.
   F. Investigate vendor reputation.
VII. Design optimum system to meet company's present and future needs.
VIII. Develop telecommunication system implementation plans.
IX. Establish a corporate telecommunications policy.
   A. Define procedures for ordering equipment and services.
   B. Define procedures for repair and maintenance.
   C. Define procedures for staff training programs.
   D. Define procedures for use of system.
   E. Define procedures for cost controls.
X. Monitor telecommunication industry changes.
   A. Monitor changes in rates, tariffs, and regulations.
   B. Monitor changes in equipment and services.
   C. Monitor changes in applications.

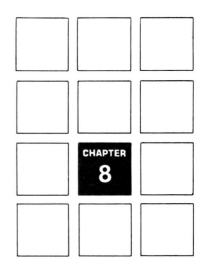

Distribution

The transfer of information between computers over phone lines will be commonplace by 1990. Advanced telecommunications technology is in place for a number of functions, including electronic banking, videotex, dial-a-game, shopping from home, and much more.

These services are facilitated by modems, which take the digital signal for transmission over a regular voice-grade telephone. The modem market is projected to grow from $40 million in 1982 to $200 million by 1987. Currently just 10 to 15 percent of home computers can handle communications like sending letters, paying bills, ordering merchandise, or receiving data. But a recent survey reported that 47 percent of home computer owners in the Chicago area plan to buy modems in the next year.

To place the significance of moving data over telephone wires in perspective requires the comparison of voice and data communications. Voice communications represents 85 percent of all traffic today, but is growing by less than 10 percent per year. Data communications is growing five times as fast and will represent over 60 percent of all line traffic by 1995.

Pacific Bell reports a new invention that can send two voice and five data channels simultaneously over a single telephone wire. One result is that customers will be able to transmit computer data without the need for a modem. This should bring advanced telecommunications and computerized home services to the mass market.

This is only the tip of the iceberg in terms of what the computer-telephone synergism can do. The telephone is becoming a semi-intelligent terminal offering features from voice synthesis to control of energy consumption. Interactive telemarketing now offers software evaluation service on line. Customers can access one- to two-page descriptions and evaluations of nearly 2000 businesses and consumer packages.

Other possible computer-phone crossovers include the use of a video display to identify the telephone numbers of incoming phone calls or the use of the computer to replace a separate answering machine.

The software industry is moving closer toward teledelivery (down-line loading) as the dominant means of delivering software. This is causing considerable alarm among retailers who fear the potential losses. As teledistribution spreads to music, games, and the video industries, losses to retailers may exceed $2 billion a year. Teledistribution eliminates warehouses and inventories. It can deliver the latest version of software to businesses and consumers. Teledelivery also offers the potential to transmit programs directly from the "author" to the customer, bypassing the publisher, distributor, and retailer. The designer of the software then retains all the profits from the program. Proponents of software teledistribution claim that it will significantly lower prices.

The biggest problem of teledistribution is the smuggling of programs and data by telephone. The current effort to control software exports is part of the Reagan administration's drive to deny the Soviets access to high technology that could be used for military purposes. Computer software and data cannot only be exported on discs and tapes but can also be sent by electronic impulses over the telephone network. It is feasible for the owner of a personal computer in Washington, D.C. to make a 5-minute call to London and export a computer-aided design program that would be useful to a weapons engineer. Pentagon analysts are searching for ways to detect illegal exports through international communications networks.

MAIL BY TELEPHONE

MCI Corporation's new service uses its long-distance telephone network to move letters around the country electronically. Taking advantage of the personal computer boom, MCI is aiming at the $8 billion per year and growing, time-sensitive mail market.

Users must have a computer terminal, personal computer, telex or TWX machine, word processor, or electronic typewriter to send and receive computer messages.

After composing a letter on the keyboard, the user "mails" it by calling a local or toll-free number to connect the modem to the MCI computer. The message is then sent over phone lines. MCI bills each user monthly for the letters sent.

The postal service's Express Mail, a relatively inexpensive overnight service, costs $10.75 and requires senders to bring letters to the post office or to special mailboxes. A three- to five-page MCI overnight letter to a nonsubscriber costs about $6 and can be sent directly from a word processor or computer terminal without someone going to a central office or calling a courier.

Electronic mail is growing by 68 percent annually with 3 million electronic mailboxes to be in use by 1987.

Voice Mail

An executive dials the number of the voice mailbox at corporate headquarters. The computer reports that there are nine messages waiting for replies. Using the telephone's Touch-tone keys, the executive quickly scans the messages for sender and purpose. Four messages require immediate action. So the executive records a response for the messages over the phone, plays them back to check for accuracy, and then forwards them to the senders' mailboxes.

With one phone call, which can be placed from virtually any telephone in the world, an executive can conduct business or touch base with the corporate office—with no callbacks. This is the capability of voice store and forward systems or voice messaging.

Telecommunications studies indicate there is less than a 25 percent chance of reaching your intended party on the first attempt. Ensuing calls result in "telephone tag." With voice messaging, response to your message can be delivered without your being there to receive it.

Extensive travel by sales staffs produces telephone tag and high credit card bills. Voice messaging can reduce the long-distance bills in sales departments.

Dectalk Mail Access

Digital Equipment Corporation introduced a product that "reads" electronic messages over the phone to authorized users. Dectalk Mail Access allows traveling businesspeople who don't carry portable computers to receive messages over phone lines. Users can phone in for electronic messages. Documents can be read over the phone by a computer.

DATA BY TELEPHONE

"If a supplier is not prepared to communicate electronically in 3 years," warns Thomas Hummer, chairman of the Automobile Industry Action Group, "he's probably not going to be able to bid on Big Four (automobile) business."

It is estimated that the paperwork between automakers and their 25,000 suppliers adds $200 to the cost of each U.S.-made car and truck. When Detroit eliminates virtually all company paperwork by 1988, it will reduce the waste from bills, orders, and requests by $2 billion a year. General Motors demonstrated its commitment to this project by purchasing Electronic Data Systems (EDS) for $2.5 billion in 1984.

Reading Meters by Phone

The New York Telephone Company has asked the State Public Service Commission to approve a plan to read utility meters by telephone. This could eliminate the door-to-door meter reader.

The service will make readings only on telephone lines that are not in use. The reading will automatically disconnect if a call comes in during a reading. Readings during the test program were 100 percent accurate and took about 2 seconds to perform. A meter can be read by dialing the last five digits of a customer's home phone number.

Electronic Newspapers

Electronic transmission of news bypasses a number of time-consuming steps in assembling a newspaper. It can eliminate composing, typesetting and text column processing, pasteup, photographing the board, and processing the negatives. Advertisers are also sending ads over phone lines to newspaper computer systems. The only thing keeping remote transmission from growing faster is the lack of a universally accepted transmission standard.

1411

The 1411 Company has developed a service that combines the features of the traditional Yellow Pages with directory assistance and offers it at a lower price. When a Houston caller requests information, the operator searches the data base and gives the caller the options over the phone. The 1411 ad copy is stored in computer memory and can be changed on 24-hours notice while Yellow Page ads are frozen for a year. In its first month of operation in the Houston area, the 1411 Company received 50,000 calls. Three months later it received 700,000 calls. The venture cost nearly $16 million to get off the ground.

Directory Express

Illinois Bell found a new way to generate extra revenue since the AT&T divestiture. They introduced Directory Express, a service that allows business customers to gain direct access to Bell's computerized directory listing. Customers can now bypass the 411 operator. This service distributes directory data to businesses for 50 percent less than the traditional directory assistance. Yet the service is projected to earn Illinois Bell almost $5 million per year.

The start-up package costs $150 and includes an identification number, password, operation manual, and training classes. The minimum monthly charge of $50 covers the first 5 hours of usage. After that, the service costs 14 cents a minute and 8 cents every time a screen is called up.

Computers Use the Phone

Some Coca-Cola machines are being equipped with a computer system that automatically places a phone call to a computer at a Coca-Cola dispensing office. The computer reports how many bottles have been sold. This allows the distributor to know when the machines need refilling without making unnecessary stops.

High-Technology Police Reports

Police officers are using portable computers and telephones to submit their reports. The St. Petersburg, Florida police department has twenty-five Tandy model 100s in the field. Officers use them to gather their report information. At the end of the day, the information is transmitted through telephone lines back to headquarters. This eliminates returning to the station an hour early to fill out reports.

Real Estate Information

Lusknet is an electronic real estate information service. By tapping into Lusknet, real estate professionals can find out not only who is lending money to whom but what is selling where, who is buying it, and what they are paying for it. What Lusknet provides are new ways of organizing, retrieving, and transmitting data. Transactions are indexed through eighteen variables, including selling price, street name, house number, neighborhood, type of zoning, type of mortgage, and the names of buyers, sellers, and lenders. Lusknet contracts for the service with more than 140 realtors, appraisers, and lenders. It costs $60 an hour to tap the data base between 8:00 A.M. and 5:00 P.M.

Telegames

AT&T Consumer Products Division and Coleco Industries are planning to distribute video games and entertainment software by telephone. AT&T is making the modems and Coleco is providing the programming. The strength of the two firms should position them as leaders in telephone-delivered games. This collaboration also allows Coleco to gain access to millions of buyers of video games and home computers who have bought systems from competitors.

Mud for Fun

The multi-user-dungeon (Mud) game links up computer users in Britain, Europe, Japan, and the United States to work and war with each other. Although home computers and networking are old news, for the first time, this game puts the two together to allow people to play against unknown adversaries from anywhere in the world. It is linked via Compunet, a British public access viewdata network, and can be tied into by a home computer and a telephone line.

WORK BY PHONE

Sales Reports

Coca-Cola USA's fountain department has transformed written reports from 250,000 retail accounts into electronic signals sent over telephone lines via portable teletransaction systems. Hand-held computers and modems have revolutionized reporting for Coke's fountain sales department. It has reduced paperwork and resulted in faster processing of sales data.

  With 250 salespeople each calling on an average of forty accounts a week, the department's data processing group processed 10,000 forms a week. This totaled more than 500,000 each year. A six-person staff was required to keypunch the data into a computer. Customer reports were produced and sent to the field sales force. Turnaround time between sales calls and the receipt of the updated route sheets was as long as 60 days. Data entry errors and bulky reports often accompanied the revised route sheets.

Teletransaction reduced Coca-Cola administrative efforts by 75 percent because data are now processed instantly and data editing occurs at the source. At the end of the business day, a salesperson connects the compiling device to a pay or home phone. A WATS line number is entered, and the data is transmitted in 60 to 90 seconds to a mainframe computer in Atlanta, Georgia. Coca-Cola USA's thousands of written sales reports have been reduced to a flurry of electronic signals sent over telephone lines across the United States.

Interactive Journalism

When reporters go on location to cover a story they can bring their readers with them. After gathering a report, they go to a pay phone, hook up their acoustic couplers, which attach to a portable computer, and they dial their numbers. The text entered on the computer is then sent to all their readers. Readers can respond with questions and comments sent through their modems and personal computers.

One problem related to the interactive nature of these reports is that readers complain about questions and answers interrupting the flow of reports. To overcome this, consider conducting two conferences. One would be a "read only" conference and contain only reports on the story—no questions allowed. The other conference would give people the chance to ask questions and discuss points.

Weather Observers

Each day, thirty-six weather observers across Illinois call a computer at the University of Illinois. Using their Touch-tone phone's keypad, they punch in weather data on the temperature and precipitation in their area. The Climate Assistance Service puts on-line daily weather collection which is still done on a monthly basis in many other states. The system presents the data in a usable form on the same day the observations are made. The accuracy of the data is double-checked by the computer.

End-to-End Automated Distribution

The Belknap Company is a supplier of quality hardware to retailers across the United States. To expand their business, Belknap developed a totally automated end-to-end distribution system. This system allows for a continual information flow between retail stores and distribution centers. Inventories are monitored and orders are placed electronically.

This distribution system furnishes instant management information and financial reports including profit margins and costs of goods sold. The distribution system integrates AT&T's UNIX PC, hand-held data terminals, and AT&T's enhanced network services.

Auto Diagnosis by Phone

On-line auto repair is Buick's new computerized diagnostic tool that finds and fixes intermittent and recurrent engine problems. The car's diagnostic connector can be plugged into a portable data recorder and linked to a remote computer over phone lines. A tape allows for delayed data transmission.

If a problem can't be solved at the dealer level, the portable data recorder connects 1981 and later model Buicks to computers at the company's Flint, Michigan, headquarters. Here's how it works: At the end of the day, a service manager removes the recorder from the car, hooks it up to a phone connected to Buick's Michigan service operation, and reruns the tape. Engineers in Flint trace the problem and relay the remedy to the dealer.

FOOD BY TELEPHONE

Drive-Through Grocery Store

A phone-in drive-through market opened in Los Angeles in May, 1983. It operates out of a 37,000-square-foot warehouse at a major intersection. This provides easy traffic access during nonrush hours.

Customers phone in their orders and pick them up a minimum of 3 hours later. A one-time $20 membership fee puts them on-line with a computer. The customer phones the order in to a computer operator, who checks the availability and current prices of the products. The operator gives the total price of the order and assigns a color-coded pickup zone where the bags will be waiting.

All transactions are done by check only. Cash and credit cards are not accepted. Customers identify themselves at the store by speaking into an identification box like those used by fast-food restaurants. They give their phone numbers as identification. They are then directed to one of the six drive-up doors so their orders can be loaded into their cars.

The warehouse operates from 4:30 A.M. to 10:30 P.M. and employs over eighty people. With the one-time membership fee comes a thirty-three-page monthly catalog listing nearly 4000 products from which to order.

Long-Distance Catering

Coastal Express Caterers of West Hartford, Connecticut began sending food by phone in 1981. They have an international list of quality caterers to prepare breakfasts, lunches, and formal dinners.

By dialing a toll-free number, customers order gourmet food, such as baskets of cheese, brunch platters, cakes, and complete dinners. A chocolate mousse cake costs about $25, a turkey dinner for two starts at $65, and a complete breakfast-in-bed package for two is $60.

Coastal Express Caterers covers fifty states and London. It is open from 9:00 A.M. to 9:00 P.M., Monday through Friday. The three-person office is lined with nearly 3000 telephone books. They handle between fifty and one hundred clients a week. Coast Express Caterers earned profits of 12 percent on revenues of over $100,000 at the end of their third year in business.

Long-Distance Liquor

800 Spirits, Inc. entered the liquor gift-giving market with a $5 million national media campaign in May, 1983. The firm's toll-free phone number, 1-800-BE THERE, tied into their initial marketing campaign, "Be there in spirit."

Liquor is delivered by some 1500 full-service retailers across the country within 24 hours of the order. All orders are purchased by credit card. The Avis Telecommunications Wizard Center supplies 200 operators for the program. 800 Spirits will soon expand to 10,000 full-service dealer networks.

Somerset Importers, marketers of Johnnie Walker Black scotch, have set up toll-free telephone booths for Father's Day in New York City. From June 15 to 17, callers talk to their fathers free of charge anywhere in the United States from British-style phone booths. Somerset covers the cost of the calls. Callers can also dial a toll-free number and have Johnnie Walker Black delivered to their dad's door.

Hamburgers by Phone

White Castle's telemarketing program is evolving into a national 24-hour business. A TV campaign by White Castle in 1982 focused on the chain's fanatical following using the theme "White Castle has the taste some people won't live without." Hamburger shipments are now easier because of toll-free calling to a telemarketing center.

Phone orders are sent by computer to their Columbus, Ohio, office, where freight bills are printed and the White Castle commissary is notified. Shipments are sent out daily, packed in dry-ice containers. White Castle ships more than 10,000 hamburgers each week.

Cookies by Phone

There is a 24-hour Girl Scout Cookie hot line in Maryland. For the first time, the Girl Scouts are using the hot line to send cookies by direct mail. The minimum phone order is six boxes at $2 per box.

Bypassing the Distribution Chain

A growing number of packaged-goods companies are changing their normal distribution channels. Companies such as Nestle's, Lipton, Sunkist, Whitman's Chocolate, and Reynolds are using catalogs and 800 numbers to sell premium-quality products directly to consumers without relying on the retailer as the middleman.

These companies are learning to sell goods by the dozen and by the case to one person at a time. This is creating a direct-marketing profit center for many packaged-goods companies. In 1983, consumers spent $45 billion shopping from home. Two-income families are proving to have disposable income but not disposable time.

For years consumers would walk into neighborhood stores and buy Whitman's chocolates. Now they are dialing a toll-free 800 number and for $25 ordering a gift tin of candy which is delivered within 48 hours.

Fast Food and Home Delivery

What could be easier than microwave dinners or drive-through fast-food restaurants? The answer is home delivery of culinary delights from chicken to pizza. Home delivery is back and serving the upscale baby-boom market that has disposable income for services. Statistics show that college students, shut-ins, and busy families also enjoy the convenience.

In Houston, Texas, Popeye's Famous Fried Chicken and Biscuits tried a home-delivery test. It was so successful that the chicken chain built twenty outlets devoted solely to home delivery. Home delivery of pizza was once again popularized as Domino's Pizza Chain began to penetrate the market.

TELEPHONE AS A MEDIUM OF EXCHANGE

By the year 1999, banking experts predict that between 25 and 50 percent of all U.S. payments will be made electronically. The growth of automated clearinghouses will have made this possible.

Companies will soon begin competing with the Federal Reserve System in processing payments between banks. In 1985, 500 million electronic transactions were executed among financial institutions. This is a small amount compared to the projected 20 billion annual electronic transactions within 15 years.

It has been the Fed's complacency which has lured new competition. When the Fed didn't respond to the needs of financial institutions, Calwestern Automated Clearinghouse Association invited bids from companies interested in entering the business. Eight companies entered and Geisco (General Electric Information Service Company) was declared the winner.

Tickets by Phone

Today, ordering tickets for Broadway shows or rock concerts requires nothing more than picking up the phone and reading numbers off a credit card or punching them in by phone. Ticket selling entered the marketplace in 1967 when Ticketron (then known as Ticket Reservation Systems) opened its first outlet in New York City.

In 1984 Ticketron, Ticket Master, and Ticket World sold more than 100 million tickets through their networks of nationwide outlets and charge-by-phone operations. The telephone makes ticket buying the ultimate buying convenience.

Quick Pay

Sears, Roebuck and Company is expanding its efforts to become a broad-based financial services company. They are now test-marketing a service for paying utility bills called Quick Pay. Available only to their credit card customers in Los Angeles, Sears allows consumers to pay utility bills by calling a phone number.

Touch-tone phones provide access to electronic tellers. Dial phones connect with operators and oral instructions are given. Sears pays the bills through its Sears Savings Bank. Funds are automatically withdrawn from subscribers' accounts at any bank. Subscribers pay a flat $3.95 per month for the service.

Sear's retailing strength provides the foundation for building their consumer-oriented full-service financial institution.

Citicorp's Portable Terminal

Citicorp is testing a palm-sized personal computer terminal that will let people around the country do their banking business without going to the bank. The portable terminal is the size of a hand-held calculator and plugs into a telephone.

This system allows bank customers to check their balances, transfer money between accounts, look up recently written checks, and, eventually, pay certain bills. Citicorp hasn't set a date for the introduction of this new service.

SUMMARY

Channels of distribution are established to transfer ownership of products or services to buyers. The rules for developing distribution channels are changing. The Information Age is defining four criteria for the effective delivery system:

1. Make feedback immediately available through quality control systems.
2. Reduce labor costs by integrating the new technology.
3. Give round-the-clock self-service as a distribution option.
4. Allow the consumer to dictate the time and place of delivery.

In an environment of intense competition, one way to reduce prices and increase market share is through disintermediation. This is the process of cutting out the middleman in the distribution system. The reduction of personnel costs, one of the major expenses involved in delivering products and services, can improve your competitive position.

Companies are investing in new distribution technology to offer self-ticketing, self-serving, self-reserving, self-ordering, and more in order to bypass the agents, brokers, manufacturers, warehousers, and retailers in the distribution process.

Delivery of products and services in the Information Age will require an investment in telecommunications to reduce the costs of labor and energy. Telephone technology will provide the next breakthrough in distribution effectiveness and efficiency.

Pricing

A price represents the value of a product or service for both the seller and the buyer. This value involves both tangible and intangible factors. An example of a tangible factor is the cost savings that comes with a purchase. An intangible factor is the peace of mind that comes from buying one brand over another.

From a broad perspective, pricing is the mechanism for allocating goods and services among potential purchasers and for ensuring competition among sellers in an open market economy. This chapter discusses how telephone technology affects a company's pricing structure. Other facets of the marketing mix also help determine an equitable value to the customer while maximizing sales and profits:

- Prices vary over the product life cycle from high at the introduction to low when attracting a mass market.
- The price can be affected by the level of customer service.
- The price can be affected by the complexity of the distribution channels.

• The sales force often affects prices when negotiating a selling price and finance terms.

Price planning is a systematic decision-making process that companies undergo to determine an equitable value to customers while maximizing sales and profits. Telephone technology is having a significant impact on price planning as it pervades the marketplace, replacing the high costs of labor and energy that influence pricing decisions.

THE TELEPHONE'S INFLUENCE ON PRICING FACTORS

Telephone technology is affecting nearly every element that is related to a company's pricing structure. In many cases, investment in technology reduces or eliminates labor costs while it expands the scope of the service or product. Pricing changes when the telephone is successfully integrated into one or more of the following categories:

• *Product-Service.*   Class, versatility, or obsolescence
• *Production.*   Orientation or method
• *Distribution.*   Channels or technological change
• *Market.*   Coverage, share, or development

Product-Service

Class.   Telephone technology can transform a high-priced custom offering into a lower-priced commodity with wide availability. The Pilots and Passengers Association of Glen Burnie, Maryland uses a toll-free phone number and a computer to match private pilots with passengers for flights along the east coast. When the cost of flying exceeded most pilots' budgets, they struck a balance: doing what they want to do (fly) with what they can afford to do (not fly as much).

In this case, passengers share the cost of operating the plane, and pilots fly at no additional cost. The passengers get where they want to go for about the same cost as driving. The pilot gets additional hours of flying time needed to upgrade a license without footing the full cost of renting and operating a plane.

Initially the service was not successful because the matches were done through a newsletter. The problem was making the matches in a timely fashion. The telephone and computer have solved this problem and turned Maryland flying from class to mass.

Versatility.   The telephone enhances another element in a company's offering—versatility. In Orlando, Florida, Valencia Community College has started "interactive audio teletraining." Instructors can teach by phone from anywhere. A computerized teleconference terminal called *the bridge* lets the teacher transmit to twenty-four locations, using a conference phone and speaker system located in each makeshift classroom. Students use desk microphones to talk with teachers and other student groups. Students participating at home use just the telephone.

Obsolescence.   The telephone can eliminate a high-priced environment to deliver a lower-priced product or service. Montgomery Ward's catalog stores are quickly becoming outmoded because of high labor costs and overhead. They are shutting down most of their 300 catalog stores in a move that could mean the elimination of at least 1200 jobs nationwide.

The Chicago-based retail company said it is converting to a direct mail-order system with a toll-free telephone number. This change in the 112-year-old company is part of a recent effort to streamline operations by adding new products and dropping unprofitable ones. Customers will order directly through the toll-free 800 number. The first catalog stores to close are in small towns that have no Montgomery Ward store.

Production

Orientation.   Telephone technology is changing the follow-up systems in dental offices. Telephone dialing systems are proving to be a cost-effective way to remind patients that they are due for their checkups. The hygienist can program the dialer to call through the patient files to remind them of their semiannual cleaning. The automatic redial features of the "busy" and "no answer" signals help the hygienist or receptionist keep track of who has been contacted. This inexpensive device provides a systematic orientation for scheduling dental patients.

Method.   The complex Internal Revenue Service (IRS) tax system requires high-priced specialists to address the tax problems of the American public. The customized service was in need of a new production method to reduce costs associated with the service. A new telephone technology, called the audio storage and dial retrieval system, was instituted to mass-produce the same message in the form of TeleTax. As a public service of the IRS, TeleTax gives recorded tax information over the telephone through recorded tapes. Local phone numbers can be called to request a list of tax topics. This system will pay for itself as major tax changes can be explained to the public without requiring additional personnel.

Distribution

Channels.   One of the greatest changes taking place in our society is known as disintermediation. This is the process of reducing the complex, high-priced distribution channels to a simple low-priced system; in other words, cutting out the middleman. Executive Books, one of America's largest wholesalers of motivational and business books, provides a convenient way to order hardcover and paperback books. By dialing 1-800-233-BOOK, anybody can buy books in volume at a reduced rate. This company circumvents bookstores and mails out orders within 24 hours. A book buyer gains immediate access to any book that is discussed by an author or reviewed on radio or television. The sale can be completed at a time when the listener or viewer may be most eager to buy. Authors find the 800 number a good way to sell books, especially when local retailers don't yet have the book in stock.

Technological Change.   Telemetering is a pilot program that uses telephone lines to automatically transmit electric, gas, and water meter readings. This program, the result of a technological change, benefits customers and utility companies through the elimination of estimated bills and manual reading of meters.

The computer can read a meter in a fraction of a second without ringing the phone. If someone is using the phone, the system waits until the line is free.

The telemetering system uses encoders supplied by the utilities, which are attached to meters and translate the readings on a meter's dial into a digital format. At the telephone switching center, a scanner and connecting equipment route all meter reading signals to and from a central host computer that directs the entire system.

Market

Coverage.   The high cost of establishing an overseas branch has been lowered by telephone technology. You can open up a branch office in Europe for $345 a month. This is what Service 800 charges for an overseas toll-free line that lets customers around the world call your office in the United States and only pay the cost of a local phone call.

Through contracts with foreign governments and leases with overseas carriers, Service 800 can provide a local phone number in any of twenty-eight countries. Competing with AT&T, Service 800 also has a new service that offers a telemarketing operation. If you advertise abroad, there can be local operators standing by to take customer orders—in twelve languages.

Share. When Comp-U-Card International wanted to expand their market nationwide, they turned to the telephone. This computerized shopping service and Bank One of Columbus, Ohio offer the benefits of computerized shopping to people who don't own computers—through a toll-free phone service. For $25 a year, Bank One issues a special Visa card that includes membership in Comp-U-Card's telephone shopping service, Comp-U-Store. A data bank lists more than 60,000 items. Discounts range from 10 to 40 percent off the suggested retail price. By calling a toll-free line and giving the model number of the item, you'll receive a price that includes tax and delivery. You can place an order or you can use the information for comparison shopping, which is what 60 percent of its members do.

Development. Telephone technology can influence prices in mature markets that have heavy competition. Telecomputers are being used to follow up on service calls to see if the product a customer recently ordered is functioning properly. Telecomputers can be programmed to call, talk, and record responses from customers. Wisconsin Bell uses a telecomputer the day an order goes into effect by following up with a call. The message says, "Hello. This is Wisconsin Bell with a recorded message. Access to your home to connect your service was not necessary. If you are still having problems, at the tone please leave your name and a brief description of your trouble. We will call you during our next business day. Thank you."

This device enables Wisconsin Bell to contact customers about troubles before they are contacted. Phone numbers are programmed, the message is recorded, then the telecomputer does the rest.

IMPROVING PRODUCTIVITY THROUGH TELEPHONE TECHNOLOGY

In general, a customer measures the price of a product or service against the relative value of its performance. The customer's perception of a price is quite subjective. One strategy for improving pricing perception by your customers is to provide a better service or product that uses less energy and less labor. Improving productivity through telephone technology can help reduce the price of products and services and enhance the price perception of the consumer.

One-Step Mortgage

Prudential Insurance Company's sophisticated telephone loan application and approval system is changing the way Americans finance their real estate. The new program connects Prudential's nationwide network of 25,000 insurance agents with their 50 million policyholders. The firm plans to generate up to $2 billion in new mortgages within its first 18 months. Quotes on fixed- and adjustable-rate mortgages will be set every weekday and made available via the firm's toll-free number.

Telecommunication, the heart of the new service, allows a home loan officer to take complete applications and provide a conditional commitment of funds, terms, and interest rates to buyers in one phone call. For the vast majority of callers, getting a loan will be handled entirely by telephone, rather than having to leave work or home to sit down with a lender. The entire country is now hooked into the phone-loan system.

The strategy was designed to cut overhead and maximize volume. By emphasizing the latest technologies Prudential has eliminated the need for a costly network of local offices.

AutoHotline

AutoHotline is a company that handles inventories for nearly half of Washington, D.C.'s 200 used car dealers. What makes this multiple listing service so unusual is that buyers shop for the used cars by telephone.

AutoHotline invested $225,000 in equipment and supplies to launch the venture. Now the computers produce lists of vehicles for sale in private driveways and on used car lots for about 350 callers a day. They service the customers who know what they want but don't have the time or patience to look for it.

A customer who calls the hot line is interviewed by a service representative as to the type of vehicle wanted. The request is coded into a computer that is programmed for make, model, year, and price range. Within 5 minutes a list of car lots and private owners who have the type of vehicle is produced. Private owners pay AutoHotline a one-time fee of $32 to list their cars until they are sold. Dealers pay a wide range of fees, depending on the number of cars they list and how quickly the vehicles are sold. The buyer pays nothing.

AutoHotline's convenience, efficiency, and low advertising costs appeal to the dealers and customers.

Self-Service Reservations

A first-of-its-kind service allows the use of personal computers to electronically order plane tickets, secure hotel rooms, and reserve rental cars. Travelers link up via ITT Dialcom Communications Service to Pan American World Airways' reservation system, which contains pricing and scheduling information for 736 airlines, 2500 hotels, and eight rent-a-car chains.

The reservation and credit information data is routed to a travel agent for delivery or directly to an airline ticket office for pickup. The charge is $19.50 per hour during the day, but there is no charge if the process takes less than 10 minutes. Computerized travel systems will be even easier to use when they can totally bypass travel agents and send tickets via electronic mail.

People Express began a service that allows a caller with a Touch-tone phone to make reservations through the company's computer, again, bypassing clerks. The service is called Pick Up and Go and callers talk to a computer. Calls are answered by a tape-recorded voice requesting the caller's telephone number, which is entered by pressing buttons on the phone. Each response is concluded by touching the button marked "#". The phone number serves as identification when the caller picks up the ticket at the airport check-in counter.

Automated Dunning

The IRS's $107 million computerized phoning system is cutting costs for tax collection. The automated dunning system is running at all twenty-one calling sites and is projected to reduce collection costs by $30 million a year and eliminate 1700 jobs. The system sets priorities and schedules and dials calls for IRS workers.

At the four test sites, the computerized phoning program closed 281,600 cases in 9 months, up from 252,000 over the same period in the previous year. The IRS collected $270.5 million, up from $212.8 million, and cut case inventory to 181,000 from 225,700. This was done with 415 employees, down from 695.

Daily Balances

When corporate finance managers call the Shawmut Bank of Boston's cash management service department, the voice that greets them is a speech synthesizer. It tells callers their exact account balances. With up to 700 callers per day making the same request, the bank searched for new options. Now each incoming call is answered by the computer and routed to one of six speech synthesizers linked to a minicomputer. Callers give their number and a password, then the voice-synthesized computer gives their balance.

INTEGRATING THE TELEPHONE INTO YOUR PRICING STRUCTURE

There is no set strategy for pricing a service or product. The most effective way to go about this exercise is to establish a test through a representative sampling of your market. A formal testing procedure starts by asking questions of current customers, prospects, salespeople, middlemen, and industry specialists. This helps to find out what is happening in the marketplace so your pricing test can be put into its market perspective. The following strategies show how the telephone can be integrated into the pricing structure.

Skim the Cream of the Market Strategy

In this strategy there is no comparable competitive product or service, but a large number of buyers. Testing a pricing strategy here is a good way to evaluate customer response and to see if competitors will enter the market.

One physician decided to stop giving free care to patient callers. He now collects $36,000 a year for phone advice, and his practice continues to thrive. After evaluating the risks of alienating patients and going against a management consultant's advice not to charge for phone consultations, he still chose to charge.

He began by charging $1 for calls at home. This was introduced by a notice on patient billings: "Effective immediately, a $1 charge will be made for telephone consultations after office hours and on weekends and holidays." Rather than receiving fewer calls at home, he received more. He then performed a time study and found that he devoted 30 percent of his office time to phone problems. He spent another hour each evening on the phone with patients.

Today the doctor charges $5 at home and $4 at the office for giving telephone advice and prescribing over 48 working weeks a year. On evenings and weekends at home, he earns an average of thirty fees weekly at $5 each, totaling $7200. At the office, he averages about twenty-five calls a day at $4 each, 6 days a week, totaling $28,000. His home and office phone charges for the year are $36,000.

He realized that there is too much time and expense involved in his telephone counseling and subscribing to give it away. He charges a premium price for his service distinctiveness. And his patients are willing to pay more because of the value they derive from his service.

Slide-Down Demand Curve Strategy

The objective of this pricing strategy is to become an efficient manufacturer at optimum volume before competitors can get entrenched. Hospitals, besieged by new competitors and pressured to cut costs, are entering a new and unfamiliar financial environment. As patient census declines and the government's new payment systems are implemented, hospitals are faced with the challenge of becoming low-cost providers of medical care in order to compete on a price basis and maintain their market share.

Cardiac Communications, Ltd. has introduced a product to help hospitals compete. It is a portable computerized system that constantly monitors the heart functions of cardiac patients and allows them to leave the hospital sooner. The system can spot abnormal rhythms and alert physicians to possible problems.

The unit consists of a 9-ounce radio transmitter worn by the patient. A briefcase-sized receiving computer, plugged into a telephone, analyzes transmissions and automatically dials the hospital when the patient has an abnormal heartbeat. Cardiologists can react immediately to ventricular tachycardias by calling patients and advising them to change medication or dispatching paramedics to the patients' homes.

The new system is automatic and requires no action on the part of the patients. Cardiac patients who are given new medication can leave the hospital early. They no longer need to remain hospitalized so the effects of new medication can be monitored. Telephone technology is keeping costs down and helping the hospital industry compete as a low-cost provider of health care services.

Competitive-at-the-Market-Price Strategy

A growing number of new lawyers are offering comparable services at lower prices, forcing established law firms to find new ways to lower their prices. The goal is to stimulate the demand for legal services among current clients.

A labor lawyer with about 500 clients has devised a list of options to help his law firm create new ways to approach the marketplace.

He introduced a "preventive maintenance" program that offers unlimited telephone advice and limited-rate services. For $200 per month clients can call to ask questions without worrying about the "meter running" for the telephone time. Another option provides up to

10 hours of legal services per month for a flat rate of $100 per hour. This allows clients to take full advantage of his expertise while problems are small.

This strategy was introduced by a letter sent to all clients. The letter listed the billing rate for the top partners and then gave the methods for cost savings. The procedure for implementing this type of strategy starts by analyzing the final price and working back to the basic costs. Customer surveys and competitive pricing structures help determine the fees.

Market Penetration Strategy

The objective of this pricing strategy is to stimulate market growth. It captures and holds the market share at a profit through low prices. A direct marketing firm imports garden tools and sells them by mail order. They have established a set of company guidelines that can apply to almost any business. Particularly germane to this strategy is guideline number 5: "The Phone Is Mightier Than the Pen."

One of their form letters that had been batted back and forth between customer service and a customer concerned an invalid American Express card. The customer's order had been held up for 2 months because of correspondence that crossed in the mail—a mail-order nightmare that came true. This company did two things. They sent her the order free. And they stopped using 22-cent stamps. "Now if there is a question, concern, nag, or doubt, we call. I do not think it costs more money, but less. It collapses the time between problem and solution, as well as eliminates paperwork," declares the president.

The use of the telephone helps reduce waste which keeps prices low. The firm also uses telephone technology to expand the market for their products.

Preemptive Extinction Strategy

The goal of this strategy is to keep competitors out of the market. The telephone is playing a key role in this strategy for the Community Referral Service (CRS).

Searching the Yellow Pages for the right contractor can be frustrating. Community Referral Service takes some of the mystery out of hiring home contractors. CRS receives hundreds of calls each month from confused homeowners looking for professional services from reliable firms.

This telephone hot line for consumers is open weekdays from 9:00 A.M.

to 4:00 P.M. Community Referral Service has an index that covers almost 500 service categories and lists over 100 contractors in the area.

The service educates consumers on how to choose contractors and how to get their money's worth. It also puts consumers in touch with contractors who offer reliable services and leads them away from the disreputable operations.

Firms listed with the Community Referral Service must be licensed and insured. They are also required to supply nine references from recent customers. Listed contractors are charged a fee everytime they are referred, which is on a rotational basis. Two firms are recommended free of charge to each caller.

The pricing structure of Community Referral Service is such that the market is unattractive to competition. As increased volume allows for lower costs, the advantage can be passed on to buyers via lower prices. The apparent low profit margins discourage potential competitors and limit competition.

SUMMARY

In order to successfully price your product or service, information about your markets, customers, competitors, and internal capabilities is required. This information helps to establish pricing guidelines.

In today's competitive environment, pricing is not a one-time decision. Rather, it is a day-by-day decision that utilizes measurable feedback systems to track the effects of pricing decisions. Most companies that approach pricing do so in several stages:

- They start by realizing their need for new pricing structures.
- They determine their pricing options.
- They design a pricing model to cope with pricing responsibilities.
- They isolate the potential problems of changing their prices.
- They establish action steps for implementing the pricing structure.
- They project the results of each pricing option.
- They establish a feedback system to monitor the pricing strategies.

Although pricing involves very little effort at implementation, it is one of the most complex functions in the marketing mix. Management needs to integrate many components in order to capitalize on pricing opportunities.

Generally, the person responsible for setting prices must know the basic costs of the products or services, then use intuition and experience to study the mathematical models, theories, and techniques. Some of the problems that may be encountered as a result of adjusting a pricing structure are as follows:

- There is a drop in sales.
- Customers interpret your effort as exploitative.
- A negative perception is created toward your product or service.
- The change in price destabilizes the market.
- The price may attract an undesirable clientele.
- Customers may become price sensitive and may not appreciate quality differences.

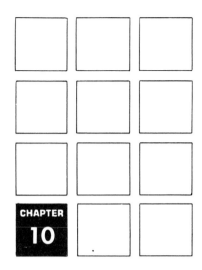

Packaging

American industry is being "repackaged" because of the growth in the telecommunications and computer industries. Since 1963, the information sector of the U.S. economy has provided nine out of ten new jobs.

Communications technologies and services have exploded as an autonomous industry, which has had a profound impact on the rest of society. Over the past 2 centuries, the U.S. economy has moved successively from agriculture to manufacturing to information processing and services. The latter now accounts for over 70 percent of the U.S. gross national product.

The structure of American business is being redefined by the dissolution of the traditional boundaries between telephone and telegraph communications, broadcasting, cable TV, and other telecommunications by the courts, the Federal Communications Commission (FCC) and Congress.

Telecommunications technology is changing buyer habits and values to such an extent that we are seeing a "new look" in traditional businesses such as law, religion, medicine, and psychological counseling.

The once humble telephone has become a powerful force in remaking American society.

FOUR LEVELS OF PACKAGING SERVICES

Any product or service can be repackaged and differentiated in today's marketplace. For example, law firms, in response to increased competition and rising costs, are repackaging themselves to distinguish their services.

Repackaging a service or product generally occurs on one of four levels: generic, expected, augmented, or potential.

Generic Legal Services

Legal services are a mix of tangible and intangible client value satisfactions. The *generic* product of the legal profession is the act of becoming a lawyer by passing a state bar exam. This gives the individual an opportunity to practice law. Passing the bar exam does not guarantee success, but you can't be a practicing lawyer without it. This is like buying a lottery ticket. Buying a ticket does not guarantee a payback, but you can't win if you don't play.

Once the generic product is established, e.g., passing the bar exam to become a lawyer, the marketplace attaches value to the product relative to its ability to help meet their needs.

Expected Legal Services

The second level of packaging legal services involves the *expected* product, which expands upon the generic product. The expected product represents to customers what is absolutely essential when they purchase legal services, such as the time frame for receiving the service, terms of the services rendered, support efforts such as specialized advice, and new applications for more cost-effective use of the generic product.

Innovations by lawyers to make their services more affordable to the average consumer are well known. These include "drugstore" lawyers with their widely advertised cut rates for simple services. However, innovations by blue-chip corporate lawyers are beginning to emerge. A Washington, D.C. law office has introduced one bold idea as an expected product for corporate clients.

Their strategy includes a letter to clients outlining seven different options which fall into two categories: preventive maintenance and fixed-fee budgeting. Their goal is to present bills that contain no surprises.

The two preventive-maintenance measures offered include unlimited telephone advice and limited-rate legal services. One way the expected product fulfills its role is by allowing clients to take full advantage of their lawyer's expertise while avoiding open-ended fees. The four levels of packaging legal services are illustrated in Figure 4.

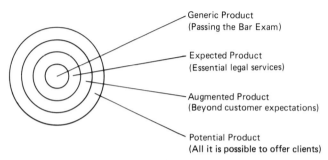

Generic Product
(Passing the Bar Exam)

Expected Product
(Essential legal services)

Augmented Product
(Beyond customer expectations)

Potential Product
(All it is possible to offer clients)

Figure 4. Four levels of packaging legal services.

Augmented Legal Services

The next step in the progression is the *augmented* product. This goes beyond giving the customer what is expected by offering services that may never have been considered.

The augmented product in the legal field exceeds the normal expectations of the buyer. Augmentation is the reflection of a mature marketplace or of sophisticated customers.

Such augmentation is being test-marketed by a subsidiary of Cigna Corporation, the insurance and financial services company. It is called Dial-a-Lawyer and is available so far only in California, New York, Pennsylvania, and the state of Washington. For a monthly fee of $8.75, legal advice by telephone is being offered to Visa and MasterCard credit card holders. Credit card holders who subscribe to this "on-line legal service" gain unlimited toll-free access to lawyers.

Subject to approval by state bar associations and state regulatory bodies, Dial-a-Lawyer, as an augmented legal service, will probably be available soon in most states.

Potential Legal Services

The final level of packaging moves into the consideration of what it is possible to offer clients and customers. The *potential* product reflects everything else that might be done to attract and hold customers.

Within legal services, potential products encompass new ideas for varying the product and service characteristics for various user segments. Only a firm's budget and imagination limit its possibilities.

A pair of Maryland attorneys have established two telephone advisory services called The Lawyer's Quill and Phone F.E.P.I. (Family Estate Planning Institute). These telephone services provide greater accessibility to their specialty practice in estate planning for clients and prospective clients.

The Lawyer's Quill is offered each Wednesday between 9:00 A.M. and 11:00 A.M. During that time the attorneys are available at no cost to answer any questions related to estate planning, including the client's work in process. Calls are limited to 10 minutes. Promotional brochures mailed to clients contain space to write out their questions beforehand and include room for answers.

The Lawyer's Quill began in the course of an estate planning session with a client who had many questions but one day expressed, "When I am at home there are questions I'd like to discuss with you but feel reluctant to call because I know I will be charged for every minute on the phone."

The companion to The Lawyer's Quill is Phone F.E.P.I., which helps people in Maryland find answers to common questions such as, "Do I need a will?" and "What is probate?" Phone F.E.P.I. offers phone-in listening to prerecorded tapes explaining estate and financial planning issues.

Phone F.E.P.I. operates from 10:00 A.M. to 5:00 P.M., weekdays. When people call, a secretary answers and asks what tape the caller is seeking. It is then played over the phone. Each recording lasts between 4 and 8 minutes. Callers may request as many tapes as they desire.

Promotional brochures provide an index of Phone F.E.P.I. tapes. Topics vary from wills to guardianship to trusts to taxes to various aspects of estate administration.

Repackaging Options

The repackaging of legal products and services occurs on four levels. Many traditional lawyers are moving beyond their *generic* and *expected* service offerings by integrating the telephone and its related technology to *augment* and *potentiate* their services.

When packaging a law firm, or other business services, consider the following options for growth and expansion:

- To promote more frequent usage by current users
- To develop more varied usage by current users

- To create new users by expanding the market
- To adapt new uses for the services

REPACKAGING IN THE PRODUCT LIFE CYCLE

Integrating the telephone into repackaging efforts is one way to extend the life of a product or service. As illustrated in Figure 5, most successful products pass through four recognizable stages:

1. *Market Development.* The introduction of a new product or service. The major tasks at this stage are to generate a demand, work out the bugs, and increase sales.

2. *Market Growth.* Characteristic of this stage is the concurrent expansion of the demand and the total market.

3. *Market Maturity.* At this stage, demand level plateaus and growth stabilizes at the replacement and new family growth rates.

4. *Market Decline.* Because of the loss of consumer appeal, the sales of the product or service begin a downward drift.

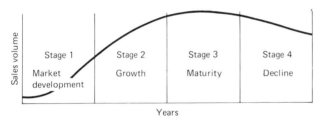

Figure 5. The product life cycle.

Perhaps the best way to view the current stage of your product or service is to try to predict the next stage and work backward. There are two major advantages to this exercise:

- It forces one to become forward-looking. Repackaging products and services focuses on meeting the needs and solving the problems of the future.

- Looking ahead enhances the present perspective. Understanding what the future will bring helps to make sense of what the present actually contains.

Talmud by Telephone

A forward-looking approach is applicable in all areas of business, including religion. In New York, the telephone has become part of a new repackaging effort. With Judaism experiencing a decline in its growth rate due to interfaith marriages and divorces, one Brooklyn rabbi has an idea for extending the continuity of the Jewish life cycle in his own community. It is called Talmud by Telephone.

Believed to be the first of its kind in the nation, the system is run from the basement of the rabbi's home and fulfills his dream to make the wisdom of the past more accessible through modern technology.

Talmud by Telephone has 1500 subscribers, many of whom are lawyers, businesspeople, and physicians. The cost is a one-time membership fee and $12 a month.

By dialing a personal number that can be used at any time without getting a busy signal, a subscriber can listen to the taped lecture in Hebrew or English. Day or night, the lecture starts promptly on the hour (except on such occasions as the Sabbath and the High Holy Days, when Jewish law forbids using the telephone).

At the pace of a page a day, 7 years are needed to finish the whole Talmud, the legal tradition of the Jewish faith. With subscriptions snowballing, Talmud by Telephone's success has led to plans for expansion in Chicago, Miami, and Los Angeles.

TeleChurch

As the demographics shift toward an aging society, the needs of the elderly are being seriously considered by Christian Education Technologies of Kingwood, Texas. Their ads read, "Pastors, multiply your contacts each day with our automatic telephone message computer. Delivers your personal message to as many as 600 homes per day. Encourage the elderly shut-ins or announce events to members and friends. Write or call for free information and leasing details."

Christian Education Technologies is helping churches integrate the telephone into packaging to help solve problems of the future. Delivering a taped message from pastors to hundreds of shut-ins each day expands the scope of any ministry far beyond that of pastors' personal visits. In addition, automatic telephone message computers offer the opportunity to announce details of special church events which will increase church awareness and attendance.

Prerecorded Prophecies

A Bethesda, Maryland man uses his telephone and recording apparatus to record religious messages. However, these are not just messages of inspiration. They are religious messages on current events which tie into prophetic scriptures. He plays the messages over his telephone answering machine for anyone who calls in.

Dial-a-Prayer

Dial-a-Prayer, a nationwide church-sponsored dial-it service, gives spiritual encouragement to callers at the press of a button. The cost is only 50 cents and is charged to your phone bill.

Church Growth Strategy

In America, 50 percent of the population is unchurched, meaning that about 120 million people are not members of a local church. As religious organizations focus on growth, the telephone will increase their options and their ability to spread the good news.

Church and "parachurch" organizations need to realize the importance of an orderly series of steps in the introduction of new technologies as they embark on a repackaging strategy. A sample of the structure for such a strategy might look something like this:

I. Observations:
   A. Within a 5-mile radius of my church, 50 percent of the people are not members of a local church.
   B. My church membership has grown at the rate of 15 percent per year for the past 5 years.
   C. Current figures show that attendance at our church services is only 60 percent of capacity.
II. Goal: Increase church membership by 25 percent per year for the next 3 years.
III. Strategy:
   A. End of first year: Expand market among current attendees.
      1. Set up a telephone computer to announce weekly events.
      2. Establish telephone discipleship outreach.
      3. Set up dial-a-prayer service for community at no charge.
   B. End of second year: Expand market among new attendees.
      1. Research needs of new attendees by phone within 48 hours.
      2. Conduct dial-a-sermon follow-up throughout the week.
      3. Dial a phone number to hear Billy Graham preach.
   C. End of third year: Find new uses.
      1. Establish a 24-hour-a-day telephone crisis hot line.
      2. Integrate a telephone computer to encourage shut-ins.
      3. Use push-button phones to vote on church issues.

ESTABLISHING A TELEPHONE REPACKAGING STRATEGY

Few businesses will be able to escape the effects of today's shifting values and expanding technologies. The telephone is even facilitating the repackaging of the medical profession. To bring about this change involves a lot of time, money, and, even more importantly, scarce technical and management resources.

A large part of the problem of successful repackaging in medicine is often simply a lack of definition. Anyone considering a repackaging strategy must understand the service or product function clearly enough to be able to define and delegate responsibility.

Repackaging Framework

A framework is required to assess the impact of the telephone and to provide a significant business advantage. Repackaging success is based on four underlying considerations of the product or service:

1. *Inventive Merit.* Creating a new combination of services
2. *Embodiment Merit.* Maximizing an idea's uses without diluting it
3. *Operational Merit.* Superseding the existing operation with the new technology
4. *Market Merit.* Increasing the market demand and the total revenue opportunities

Repackaging a Medical Practice

Repackaging the busy medical practice of four orthopedic surgeons required a balanced appraisal of all four of these criteria. When a group of orthopedic surgeons in Annapolis, Maryland converted its manual billing system to a computerized system, patients' phone calls kept the office bookkeeper busy all day long.

By analyzing the nature of the calls, it was shown that 90 percent of patient inquiries were seeking answers to the same question. So a telephone answering machine was installed with a 1-minute message informing the callers that all patients receive a bill and explaining how the computerized billing system works.

If the patient required personalized attention, calls were taken directly by the bookkeeper between 9:00 A.M. and 12:00 P.M. After these hours, patients could leave their names, phone numbers, and the nature of their problems on the recording system. This allowed the bookkeeper to call the patients back the next day.

This telephone answering procedure benefited both the patients (they learned the new computerized billing system and got questions answered) and the medical staff (they could get their office work done and still serve their patients' needs).

In response to problems created by the trend toward more athletics, the surgeons installed a sports injury hot line. Though some patients have to wait up to a month for consultation on medical problems, same-day medical diagnoses are arranged through the hot line. This has become advantageous for high school athletic coaches. The direct line into the physicians' office allows the coaches' questions about students' athletic injuries to be answered without waiting.

Medical information is also instantly accessible for these surgeons. Through a phone call, they can dial into the American Medical Association's (AMA) main computer, which is now available in 250 cities nationwide. The physicians simply dial up the menu on their computer. The terminal screen shows a list of medical topics. The vast data bank provides not only facts about drugs and diseases but also information about medical procedures, legislative updates, statistics, and AMA topics.

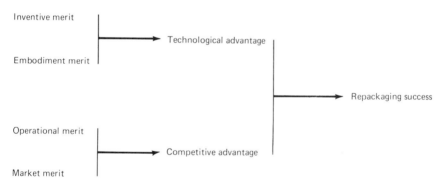

Figure 6. Framework for evaluating the validity of a repackaging strategy.

New Medical Technologies

The telephone is proving to be a real lifesaver for patients. Figure 6 shows how new technology and good business practices bring repackaging success for doctors. For example, physicians can now beam computerized images of brain scans over telephone lines. The system, designed by British Telecom, allows neurosurgeons to diagnose patients from halfway around the world.

Lifeline Systems, Inc. enables medically risky individuals to live at home rather than be closeted in hospitals or nursing homes at great expense. Subscribers wear push-button devices on their wrists that can place a telephone call for help to medical resources.

Another option for the elderly is a time-and-alert system that automatically summons help. If the timer is not reset during the normal course of daily activities—perhaps by opening a refrigerator door or flicking off a light—it will dial for help through a telephone line.

Greater acceptance of home medical monitoring is occurring. This may be due in part to the increased number of similar electronic products now found in the home, such as telephone answering machines and burglar alarm systems. The market merit of such products points to repackaging success. In the year 1999, when more than 25 percent of the population will be over 65 years of age, these types of services will be quite popular.

Medical Hot Lines

Medical information for patients over the telephone is becoming increasingly accessible through information services and medical hot lines. Tel-Med Health Information offers as a public service over 200 tape-recorded messages on health and medical problems from arthritis to heart disease. It is accurate, reliable, and convenient to use. Tel-Med, which is offered by hospitals, helps people know more about health problems, recognize early signs of illness, and remain healthy. Tel-Med operators play tapes requested by number, offering the message in the privacy of the patient's home. Each tape lasts about 3 minutes.

Medical hot lines, on the other hand, are becoming an easy way to obtain specialized information. The breast cancer hot line provides information for the consumer about breast cancer.

A new hot line offers travelers medical advisory information. The Health-alert hot line by HealthCare provides a worldwide health forecast, monitoring health, weather, and political news in more than 100 countries through a 24-hour-a-day toll-free phone number.

Just as people depend on weather forecasts before leaving home, they can call for health forecasts before leaving on a trip. Each week Health-Care, a major supplier of health insurance, makes a 2½-minute recording with medical alerts and political briefs, usually focusing on the "hot spot" of the week. The information is supplied by the Centers for Disease Control in Atlanta, Georgia, the World Health Organization, and the State Department. The toll-free number is 1-800-368-3531.

Telephone Medical Consultation

MidPeninsula Health Service (MHS), founded 6 years ago under the leadership of a Stanford preventive health specialist, currently serves over 4200 subscribers.

MHS minimizes "redundant and unnecessary tests and examinations," prescribes drugs sparingly, teaches people to take responsibility for their own health, and relies on the telephone to a great extent.

Statistics show that one-third of MHS members are over age 50 and one-fourth are over 65—presumably vulnerable to continuing medical problems. Subscribers use just 30 percent of the amount of prescription drugs taken by other Americans. Another statistic, however, may be even more telling. The MHS staff of three full-time physicians talks by telephone to patients four times as often as physicians in private practice.

Free, prolonged telephone consultations are the MHS lifeline. The American Medical Association's word on telephone consultation is contrary. It is a matter of degree. Conversations by telephone can be useful as an adjunct to face-to-face office visits, but they are not a substitute. Note the four considerations in assessing MHS's merits:

1. *Inventive Merit.* Four times greater telephone use than the average is a unique approach to providing medical service.

2. *Embodiment Merit.* Unlimited free telephone consultations seem to work because of subscriber membership format.

3. *Operational Merit.* Immobility of elderly is overcome by the telephone which increases doctor accessibility to patient.

4. *Market Merit.* About 70 million people age 65 and over by 1999 means practice is positioned to meet needs of the elderly.

MidPeninsula Health Service should experience strong growth. As long as the quality of medicine is acceptable to the needs of the patients and meets the standards outlined by the American Medical Association, the number of subscribers for this type of service will most probably increase.

Seven-Step Packaging Plan

The repackaging strategy to introduce the telephone into a medical practice should follow seven basic steps:

1. *Analyze.* Analyze the overall needs of the population being served and the current strategy to meet these needs.

2. *Explore.* Explore the telephone options which are currently being used or considered in medicine and other industries.

3. *Screen.*   Screen the repackaging options by weighing the technology and the market to determine their efficacy.

4. *Propose.*   Propose repackaging the idea by converting it into a concrete recommendation.

5. *Develop.*   Develop the idea into a model of a working service or product.

6. *Test.*   Test the repackaged service or product in the marketplace to confirm its validity.

7. *Rollout.*   Commercialize the idea. Make it widely available.

HOW TO INCREASE YOUR CHANCES
FOR REPACKAGING SUCCESS

Success in repackaging a product or service is hardly automatic. In fact, most efforts are failures, resulting in the waste of time, money, and human resources.

Within a company, the packaging effort often gets lost among the daily activities of maintaining the business. However, problems that arise in formulating a packaging strategy can be traced to three basic sources:

1. *Classification.*   Determine the type of attention required for the repackaging effort.

2. *Coordination.*   Assure continuity in the design and implementation of the packaging strategy.

3. *New Knowledge.*   Provide new information and feedback on the packaging strategy.

The field of psychological counseling is experiencing rapid growth in repackaging services through increased use of the telephone. The market needs are shifting, and telephone technology is proving to be a valid way to meet these shifting needs. It is important to classify and analyze the market and technological changes to improve the chances for packaging success.

Market Shifts

A significant behavior change in our society is the proliferation of teddy bears. The popularity of these fuzzy creatures with both adults and children has created Care Bears, specialty teddy bear stores, and teddy bear festivals.

Psychiatrists refer to the teddy bear as a transitional object that helps a child face a strange new world. Thus one can infer that an increased interest in teddy bears is evidence that there is more anxiety in our society.

Many adults, however, have abandoned the teddy bear for more "mature" crutches to relieve anxiety. They are turning to the consumption of stress-relieving substances: alcohol, tranquilizers, marijuana, and cocaine.

Psychiatric help is also in great demand. Admissions to private psychiatric hospitals have been rising even at a time when hospital utilization has been falling.

The increased teddy bear population and the need for psychiatric services seem to be signals of an over-stressed society. The proliferation of creatively packaged psychological services confirms these observations.

Dial-a-Counselor

Dial-a-Trance was introduced by a hypnotherapy clinic in Chicago. A 5-minute recorded message is played free to callers, day or night.

In the first month of operation, more than 6000 calls were received. The peak hour of operation is between 10:00 P.M. and 11:00 P.M. when people are trying to go to sleep. This first-of-its-kind service is also designed to help people quit smoking, stick to a diet, or simply cope with daily stress.

On the other hand, telephone hot lines have been providing counseling for some time. But now the practice has a new element—money. SOS Doctors in California is staffed with doctors and psychologists to handle telephone counseling. The fee is $55 for a half-hour consultation.

A prospective patient calls the SOS line and is asked by the receptionist for a credit card number. SOS then pages one of the staff who calls back within the hour. If callers lack the money, they are referred to one of the crisis hot lines or to one of the sliding-scale clinics.

The advantage of such a service is obvious for shut-ins, very busy executives, or those wishing for anonymity. However, the major drawback of the diagnostic therapy by phone is that up to 75 percent of the information normally exchanged by the doctor and the patient is through nonverbal communication, which is absent when diagnosis is done by phone.

Adults aren't the only ones affected by the stresses of society. An innovative form of "cookies 'n milk" telephone counseling, called The Kid's Connection, was set up in 1983 to help preteens get through tough times of loneliness, boredom, or worry.

The Kid's Connection is called a "warm" line rather than a hot line so that children do not feel they need a crisis to justify calling. It targets kids who have outgrown day care and sit at home by themselves waiting for their parent(s) to come home from work.

The three staff counselors (paid about $10,000 per year each), receive as many as seventy-five calls per week. Most calls are a way to fight boredom. And to relieve boredom, the counselors offer suggestions from the agency's list of fifty pastimes.

To classify the psychological service examples, they are placed into a matrix which crosses their technological newness and market newness (see Figure 7).

	Increasing Technological Newness ⟶			
	Service Objectives	No Change of Technology	Improved Technology	New Technology
No market change	—		Reformation	Replacement
Strengthened market	Remerchandising		Improved product {SOS Doctors}	Product line extension
New market	New uses		Market extension {Kid's Connection}	Diversification {Dial-A-Trance}

(Increasing Market Newness — vertical axis label at left)

Figure 7. Technological-newness—market-newness matrix for psychological service examples.

Packaging Success Factors

The best way to increase the chances for success in repackaging a business by using the telephone is to follow these steps:

1. Establish objectives to be completed in each phase of the repackaging effort.

2. Establish checklists for each phase of the repackaging effort.

3. Establish one individual to be responsible for the entire program.

4. Establish an interdepartmental reporting relationship so coordination of steps can be promoted fully.

5. Consolidate, summarize, and evaluate all repackaging proposals under consideration.

6. Establish in advance evaluation criteria for all repackaging decisions.

The people responsible for the repackaging strategy must fulfill their obligations in order to ensure success.

1. The originator of the repackaging idea participates in all phases of the project until it is fully established. (The only people who really get things done in business are monomaniacs with a mission.)

2. The person responsible for marketing the new packaging effort also participates fully in establishing the project.

3. The person responsible for development of the telephone technology participates in formulating design objectives and continues to be involved through the testing phase.

SUMMARY

It is not enough just to be competitive in the Information Age. As market values shift and technology cultivates obsolescence, creativity and adaptability will be the catalysts to repackage businesses, industries, even societies.

The integration of the telephone to solve problems of the marketplace will generate techniques to hold customers and penetrate new market segments. Repackaging a product or service through the use of the telephone often requires the shedding of convention and conviction. Combinations of disparate ideas can capture the attention of the marketplace. For example, the most sought-after phone number in New York these days is the unlisted number for *High Society*'s centerfold hot line, commonly known as dial-a-porn.

Since it began in February, 1983, the X-rated tape has received as many as 500,000 calls a day. About 150 companies nationwide advertise "telephone sex," with some offering live conversations lasting about 15 minutes and costing $30—charged to MasterCard or Visa. This combination of telephone and sex grosses up to $3 million per year for *High Society* magazine and up to $9 million a year for the phone company.

The point is that anything in today's market can be repackaged and differentiated. The challenge to create appropriate combinations of technology, products, and services invariably brings about desired results. The technology is changing so rapidly that it is nearly impossible to adequately prepare for it.

A "survival strategy" for businesses might look something like this:

I. Become a well-informed communications generalist. Gain a good grasp of the principles and practices of the new technologies. Add to that a broad background in problem-solving through creative strategies.

II. Build a strong foundation of creative technology applications within the marketing mix (promotion, advertising, prospecting, selling, research, services, products, distribution, pricing, and packaging).

III. Harness the talents of technical experts to combine the best features of the technologies into programs focused on:
   A. Efficiently canvassing your most likely respondents
   B. Maintaining accurate records on these respondents
   C. Improving the accessibility of your products and services to these respondents
   D. Enhancing product and service delivery while expediting the transfer of funds

It is the well-informed communications generalist, with the aid of technicians, who will quickly adapt to the changes and succeed in repackaging for tomorrow's marketplace.

REPACKAGING CONSIDERATIONS

Repackaging a product or service by integrating the telephone is a complex task. To minimize risks and increase chances for success, companies should analyze the business factors influenced by the telecommunications system.

1. Business planning
   - Have you included your phone system in your 5-year plan?
   - What role does your telephone system play in your company?

2. Marketing
   - What percentage of sales does your telecommunications expense account for?
   - Is your telecom system adequate for your market share?

3. Capital planning
   - Which telecom equipment can help you cut costs and increase sales?
   - Can you relate capital purchases to return on investment to help set priorities?

4. Financial management
   - Can your financial structure expand your telecommunications system?
   - What are your options to raise equity to improve your telecom system?

5. Budgeting
   - Do you have a formal telecom budget for the next 12 months?
   - How do your budgeted costs compare with your actual telecom costs?

6. Accounting
   - Do you get monthly accounting statements on your telecom system?
   - Do you account for taxes, depreciation, and system's financial analysis?

7. Employee relations
   - Have you chosen the right telecom system for the right jobs?
   - Do employees have the telecom equipment needed to do their jobs?

8. Customer relations
   - How do you use telecommunications to respond to customer desires?
   - How do you use telecommunications to resolve customer complaints?

9. Operations
   - Do you have a telecommunications operation manual?
   - Has each telecom system use been examined for cost-effectiveness?

10. Cost controls
   - Do you implement cost accounting measures to minimize telephone waste?
   - Have you considered long-distance alternatives to reduce costs?

11. Quality control
   - How does your telecom system enhance the quality of your services?
   - Do employees suggest ways to improve your telecom system?

12. Inventory management
   - Do you keep an exact inventory of your telecom system?
   - Is your telecom system utilized to manage corporate inventories?

13. Maintenance
   - Do you have a planned telecom maintenance program scheduled?
   - Do employees have a procedure to register for equipment servicing?

14. Promotion
    • How do you interface your telecom system into your promotions?
    • Is your company name tied into your telephone number?

15. Packaging and design
    • Is your telephone system interfaced into your products and/or services?
    • Does your packaging make your products and/or services "smarter"?

16. Administration
    • Have you established and enforced clear and fair telecom policies?
    • Are telecom materials, information, and records well organized?

17. Information
    • Is your telecom system a business intelligence system?
    • How do you move information through your telecom system?

18. Asset management
    • Are your telecom system's resources being fully utilized?
    • How can you change the telecom structure to improve its value?

19. Management improvement
    • How do you plan to improve your telecom management skills?
    • How do you analyze your telecom management weaknesses?

20. Distribution
    • Do you utilize your telecom system to send mail and data?
    • Have you considered your telephone to be a medium of exchange?

21. Prospecting
    • Do you interface your telecom system to aid your prospecting efforts?
    • Have you considered telecomputers for lead generation and prospecting?

22. Research
    • Do you use telephone interviews to provide accurate samplings?
    • Does your sales staff collect research data from consumers by telephone?

23. Advertising
- Do you utilize the telephone as an advertising response mechanism?
- Do you maintain telephone support advertising (e.g., Yellow Pages)?

24. Sales
- Do you cut sales costs by selling marginal accounts over the phone?
- Do you stretch sales budgets by replacing face-to-face visits with phone calls?

25. Products
- Do you have vendors provide you with new telecom product data?
- Which products can interface with your telecom system to enhance it?

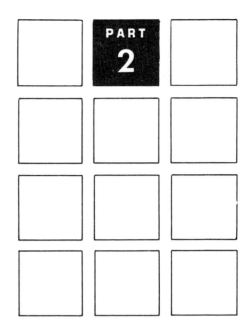

PART
2

Looking
to the
Future

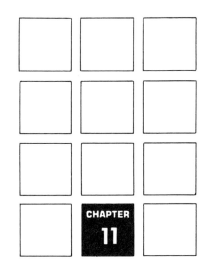

CHAPTER

11

Creating a New World

THE TELEPHONE REVOLUTION

American revolutions occur about once every hundred years. The first one took place in 1776 when King George III was ousted. The second American revolution started a century later when farms became cities and transformed America from an agricultural to an industrial economy. Railroads and highways to transport people and products were characteristic of this second revolution.

The third American revolution has begun right on schedule. This one moves information on highways of glass. A quarter million phone conversations, data, and television pictures are now being transported through bundles of glass wires called fiber optics.

This third revolution involves telecommunications and affects every American who picks up a telephone, switches on a television, or logs on a computer. This revolution began with a quiet trip to the library by a perceptive and persistent entrepreneur.

BREAKING UP A MONOPOLY

In 1969 William McGowan visited the public reading room of the Federal Communications Commission (FCC) in Washington, D.C. There he found that the FCC had granted legal monopolies to provide local telephone service. What intrigued McGowan, however, was what he did not find.

"I realized that AT&T had never been granted a monopoly on long distance," McGowan recalls. "They just evolved into it. There was no piece of paper to show that AT&T had a monopoly on long distance."

That realization led McGowan and his venture, Microwave Communications (MCI), to apply for an FCC license as a "specialized common carrier" using modern microwave technology. Once evidence was presented to the Justice Department that AT&T executives conspired to put MCI out of business, in direct defiance of the FCC, a civil investigation began.

In 1974, MCI, a company with 20 employees and sales of $30,000 in the previous year, filed a $5.8 billion antitrust suit. Six years after the suit was filed, a $600 million judgment was rendered. In 1985, an appeals court fixed a new figure and awarded MCI $37.8 million. Nonetheless, McGowan's business had mushroomed into a $2 billion per year enterprise and brought about the dissolution of the largest monopoly in American business.

It was a case of David (William McGowan, chairman of the board of MCI) slaying Goliath (AT&T, which spent nearly $300 million in legal fees battling the antitrust suit), which started a revolution in telecommunications. Rather than five stones and a slingshot, it was a 159-page opinion by Federal Judge Harold Greene that felled the giant, AT&T.

American Telephone and Telegraph (AT&T), known for generations as Ma Bell, had sales of $65.7 billion in 1982. However, in July 1983 Judge Greene ruled that the communications giant be split off into seven independent units. The court order totally restructured AT&T. When AT&T agreed to divest its local operating units to settle their government antitrust suit, it began the largest corporate break-up in history.

The ruling had far-reaching implications: AT&T had to turn over the blue and white telephone logo to newly independent local phone companies; only Bell Laboratories and foreign operations could continue using the name; AT&T had to change the name of its American Bell subsidiary which offered a full line of communications products; AT&T was required to assign its telephone equipment patents to the operating companies so they could order communications components from other suppliers; and AT&T was directed to help local phone companies recover the estimated $2.6 billion that it will cost to provide equal-quality access to long-distance carriers like Sprint and MCI, which compete with AT&T.

Dismantling AT&T involved restructuring the assets, rights, and obligations of an enterprise with 3,234,677 stockholders, 1,009,817 employees, and a network of nearly 1 billion miles of wire and cable carrying more than 600 million calls each day.

The break-up of AT&T is changing the way every American obtains and uses a phone. Highlights of the new phone product and service options are as follows:

1. *Options to Buy.*   All local Bell companies offer telephones to be purchased rather than leased. Customers are encouraged to do their own wiring and telephone installation.

2. *Continuing to Lease.*   Customers can continue to lease as long as there are still phones to lease. Phone companies are prohibited from replenishing their supplies of leased phones. Most likely, consumers will buy a phone, either from the phone company or from retailers who sell phones.

3. *Equipment Repair.*   Once a phone is bought, it will be repaired for a fee, either where you purchased it or at a repair shop.

4. *Local Rates.*   Rates for local services have risen by as much as 40 percent and even more in isolated rural areas.

5. *Long-Distance Services.*   Rates for long-distance service will continue to drop by as much as 40 percent as consumers and businesses are offered a choice between long-distance carriers like AT&T, MCI, and Sprint.

In the current American revolution, telecommunications is providing new hope to replace the failed expectations of another much heralded revolution—the nuclear industry. A Yale graduate aspiring to a career as an energy policymaker sought the counsel of Victor Gilinsky, the longest-serving member of the Nuclear Regulatory Commission. He talked earnestly to Gilinsky about nuclear and solar power, coal, oil, gas, cogeneration, and more. He asked if he was making a mistake going into the energy field.

Gilinsky, 50, known as the commission's tough regulator, responded, "Yes, you are making a mistake. Energy is out. Telephones are in. Go into telephones." Telecommunications has captured the promise that nuclear power seemed to hold a generation ago.

NEW TRENDS

A few of the trends and characteristics created by the telecommunications revolution include mobility, integration, pulsing, and satellites.

Mobility

Within the next decade, mobility will be enhanced as phone service becomes more affordable to millions of people. Travelers are placing calls from planes, trains, boats, and cars. Paging services will become more widespread. In addition to tone and audio messages, these paging devices will print out financial data, news, and industry bulletins.

Integration

One of the more profound trends to ponder is the ability to own your own phone number for life. The implications of such network integration are staggering. From a mobile car telephone in New York, for example, you could communicate by voice, data, or facsimile to any other fixed or mobile phone in the world.

Such a network allows a variety of interactive banking and retailing services, provides accessibility to a wide range of data bases, provides home security alarm systems, and delivers newspapers and magazines to subscribers through a computer terminal and printer. Computers and phones are being fused together so tightly that they are now almost indistinguishable.

Pulsing

The nerve pathways of this burgeoning telecommunications grid are strands of ultrapure glass as thin as human hair, known as fiber optics. Already in place is 30,000 miles of half-inch cable containing optical fibers running between New York and Washington, D.C. The link carries 240,000 simultaneous conversations—more than twice as many as can be carried by copper cable ten times as thick. Copper wires can carry 5000 characters per second. Satellite channels can transmit 100,000 characters per second. The fiber-optic technology can carry 3 million characters per second. This transmission capacity is made possible by laser light pulses that turn on and off 90 million times a second. Light wave communications will reach into homes and offices, delivering TV and radio entertainment, computer programs, video games, teletex messages, and two-way conduits, all through a single optical cable.

Satellites

Another characteristic of the new environment is the mushroom-shaped dish antennas seen atop skyscrapers and in suburban backyards. These dishes make satellite communications possible. Satellite carrying capacity has increased more than a hundredfold since the first carriers of the early 1960s. At an American Express company center, for example, a combination of satellites and phone links approves 250,000 credit transactions a day from around the world, in an average of 5 seconds or less. Computerized materials are routinely sent by satellites by companies. Data that would ordinarily take 31 hours (1860 minutes) by land phone lines can be transmitted in 12 minutes by satellite. The latest generation of Intel Sat VI Satellites carries more than 33,000 simultaneous phone conversations plus two TV channels between the United States and Europe.

IT'S NOT JUST A TELEPHONE ANYMORE

Credit for developing the Information Society belongs to AT&T as much as to IBM or anyone else in the information-communications business. By 1943, Bell Laboratories had more patents in the field than any other firm. But in a 1956 consent decree the Justice Department stated that AT&T could manufacture computers only for its own operations.

Now this has changed. Effective January 1, 1984, the divestiture nullifies that 1956 decree and frees AT&T to sell computers, software, and services to anyone. AT&T's plans to exploit this opportunity range from small home devices to microcomputers and all the network links in between. The new telephones will eventually include an attached terminal or a personal computer.

"Most people's home computer will not be an Apple or an IBM," according to Herb Dordnick, professor at the University of Southern California's Annenberg School of Communications. "It will be a telephone with a computer terminal. This will allow people to tap into computerized information sources."

Many people underestimate the importance of the telephone. It is the telephone's largely unrealized social role that affirms this observation. Teenagers consider the telephone second only to face-to-face meetings as a source of entertainment, ahead of television and radio. Its familiarity makes the phone a perfect tool to prepare them for the Information Age.

AT&T's strategy for entering into the office automation marketplace also centers around the telephone. While most of its competitors introduce new computers, AT&T is using the telephone to get its foot in the door.

Telephones are no longer just headsets and cradles. AT&T and a few competitors sell digital multiline private branch exchange (PBX) systems. The office now becomes its own in-house telephone company. Call switching is done internally instead of at external switching stations.

The new PBX systems work in the digital world (where voice is carried in discrete units or bits) rather than in the old analog one (where voice is carried as continuous waves.) This means that PBX systems can be hooked up to other digital equipment: terminals, personal computers, even large mainframe computers.

This technological breakthrough allows transmission of voice and data over a single telephone line. An executive, for example, can discuss an annual report that shows up on his screen while talking to a colleague who has the same report on her screen, all from the same piece of equipment on their desks.

The merging of voice and data points to the PBX as the hub of the automated office of the future. This is one of the major reasons why International Business Machines (IBM), with sales of $34.4 billion in 1982, paid $228 million to acquire 15 percent of the Rolm Corporation, a major producer of the PBX technology.

Types of Communications Networks

- *Voice Networks.*   Including local and long-distance telephones
- *Data Networks.*   For transmission of computerized data
- *Message Networks.*   Such as telex
- *Facsimile Networks.*   To send images
- *Electronic Mail Systems.*   To route and store pages of text or data

Alexander Graham Bell had no idea he was doing it, but in 1876 along with the telephone he invented the first computer terminal. By using a mix of old and new technology, it is becoming increasingly easy to use the phone as a computer terminal. Punching the buttons on a Touch-tone phone can access the data base of a mainframe computer to receive a report as easily as asking for it with the spoken word.

The enduring value of the telephone is evident, even a century after its introduction. The telephone is facilitating the process of cutting out the middleman, known as disintermediation. Automated voice recording systems are eliminating the greatest expense in dispensing information by phone: paying the operator who calls up data on a traditional terminal. Disintermediation occurs as a system's stored information is indexed by simple numerical codes. Callers identify the kinds of information they desire by punching in a code or a series of codes. This produces an "oratory" of specific, timely information.

A New Social Order

The telecommunications revolution is altering consumer behavior. As much as 50 percent of all Christmas purchases are now made by telephone. With crowded stores, limited service, frequently slow mail delivery, and a general wariness of the costly door-to-door sales approach, the speed and convenience of the telephone is positioning it as the friendly agent of change.

Holiday season shopping by phone has been facilitated by AT&T. The total of inbound 800 numbers on which customers placed orders or made reservations rose 170 percent between 1977 and 1982. The number of outbound WATS (wide-area telecommunications service) lines, by which many companies contact customers, grew 71 percent over the same period.

Of the three major technological innovations (the telephone, the computer, and the credit card) developed during the current revolution, the telephone has had the most impact on the new social order.

The telephone technology that everyone learned to use at an early age is bringing about this third American revolution. By 1988, the global telecommunications marketplace is expected to evolve into an $88 billion free-for-all. With its complete market penetration, computer integration, and ability to transfer funds electronically, the telephone has the durability and flexibility to lead the revolution.

Forces of change (inflation, regulatory pressure, antitrust actions, market saturation, and the push of technology) are moving us into a new era. We are entering the Information Age where the predominant method of communication is electronic. The telecommunications industry, responsible for information delivery, is now being restructured into four separate businesses:

1. The installation, maintenance, and leasing of equipment on the customer's premises
2. The traditional monopoly of providing local telephone services
3. Manufacturing and supplying of equipment for the industry
4. The long-haul movement of information

Talking by telephone still accounts for at least 85 percent of what is considered telecommunications. In the Information Age, electronics will also move text, data, images, and pictures around the world via satellites and fiber optics with greater speed than could have ever been imagined (see Figure 8).

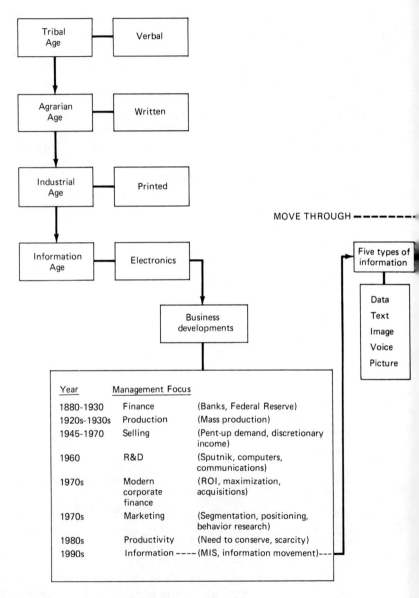

Figure 8. Business 1990: marketing and technology interfaced to move information. *(Copyright © Foresight and Planning, 1983.)*

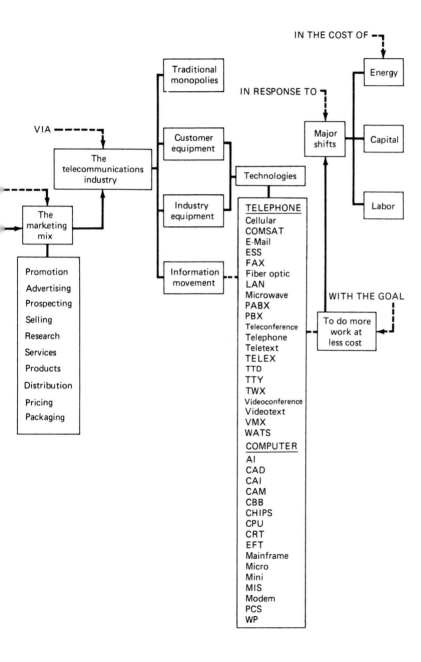

IN THE COST OF

Energy

IN RESPONSE TO

Capital

Major
shifts

Labor

VIA

Traditional
monopolies

The
telecommunications
industry

Customer
equipment

Technologies

The
marketing
mix

Industry
equipment

Promotion
Advertising
Prospecting
Selling
Research
Services
Products
Distribution
Pricing
Packaging

Information
movement

WITH THE GOAL

To do more
work at
less cost

TELEPHONE
Cellular
COMSAT
E-Mail
ESS
FAX
Fiber optic
LAN
Microwave
PABX
PBX
Teleconference
Telephone
Teletext
TELEX
TTD
TTY
TWX
Videoconference
Videotext
VMX
WATS
COMPUTER
AI
CAD
CAI
CAM
CBB
CHIPS
CPU
CRT
EFT
Mainframe
Micro
Mini
MIS
Modem
PCS
WP

TRAITS OF THE NEW TELECOMMUNICATIONS ENVIRONMENT

Developments in electronics, computer technology, and telecommunications are radically altering consumer behavior and the business environment. Innovations are happening so quickly that some state-of-the-art equipment seems practically obsolete by the time its marketing brochures are printed.

The same problems face all businesses: how to improve productivity, reduce overhead, and increase profits. Yet executives will be forced to answer these questions as they find themselves in a new business context marked by the following ten characteristics (see Figure 9):

1. Ease of Entry.   The technology explosion has launched a myriad of new companies, many aimed at improving office and business operations. With changing needs dictating the office structure, many companies are finding that the leap into telecommunications technology requires very little effort. It is this ease of entry that is allowing many companies to increase their productivity. With 44 million business phones in place, the telecommunications infrastructure already exists. The revision of corporate marketing strategies is often a matter of integrating the new technology to create a communications strategy.

For nearly a century, telecommunications equipment manufacturers carved out cozy relationships with their telephone and telegraph administrations. Torn apart by deregulation, new companies are emerging with new products and services to create a wider choice of telecommunications services. Customers are placing more demands on their telecommunications systems as they realize that to excel in the Information Age, more and more office functions will require automation.

Users can now shop for the best products at the best prices with the best marketing and technical support ever offered. Five years ago only two long-distance companies competed with AT&T. Now there are more than 200 companies offering such services. It has never been easier to enter the new telecommunications environment.

2. Minimum Start-Up Costs.   Perhaps the fear of spiraling costs has kept many companies from developing a new communications strategy. Often all that is needed to begin accessing information services is a Touch-tone telephone (not rotary) which can be purchased for as little as $50.

If a microcomputer already exists at home or at work, a $60 modem opens up a world of teledelivery. The modem links a phone and

MARKETING MIX

TELECOMMUNICATION TRAITS	Promotion	Advertising	Prospecting	Selling	Research	Services	Products	Distribution	Pricing	Packaging
Ease of entry										
Minimum start-up costs										
Integrates new technology										
Changes the nature of information										
Speeds up flow of information										
Mass to information ratio reversed										
Enhances market responsiveness										
Brings market to consumer										
Consumer controlled delivery										
Integrates electronic payment										

Applications	Source	Applications	Source
☐		☐	
☐		☐	
☐		☐	
☐		☐	
☐		☐	
☐		☐	
☐		☐	
☐		☐	
☐		☐	
☐		☐	
☐		☐	
☐		☐	
☐		☐	

Figure 9. Telecommunications applications audit.
(Copyright © Foresight and Planning, 1984.)

computer to hundreds of data bases and thousands of computer networks. Data can be transmitted directly by dialing the telephone.

To make a company's service more accessible to clients, a WATS line can be installed. The cost for such a service is about $150 per line plus the cost of the incoming calls.

The use of 900 numbers is growing quickly. Interaction over a television program gives the American people an opportunity to express themselves. On October 28, 1980, the ABC television network aired the presidential debate between incumbent Jimmy Carter and Ronald Reagan. A total of 696,429 viewers called in their vote as to the winner of the debate. This poll was set up through the television network for a flat fee of only $25.

Student truancies at Stagg High School caused $2 million in revenue to be withheld from the school by the state. An automatic dialing machine was purchased to alert parents when their children were skipping classes. The project cut absenteeism by 10 percent—paying for the machine in the first month.

3. Integrates the New Technology.   Perhaps the greatest marriage ever is between the computer and the telephone. The phone has become smarter and more versatile. Technological innovations ranging from push buttons to satellite transmission to automated dialing to branch switching have transformed the telephone from a "chat with Aunt Alice" into a technological workhorse. The office phone system has all the capabilities of a telephone company. And now the phone has the power to transmit data anywhere in the world, at any time, in a fraction of a second, at a cost less than sending it by mail.

4. Changes the Nature of Information.   The most basic function of the marketplace is the gathering and disseminating of information. Behind every transaction is the exchange of information. An item's price is only one part of the product's information. More information is being built into products through design, utility, technology, and quality.

Information is becoming more powerful as its nature is being transformed by telecommunications. Talking on the phone, voice transmission, is now only one facet of telecommunications. Data, text, image, and video transmission are all providing more input, resulting in wiser decisions, better-built products, fewer wasted resources, and lower prices.

5. Speeds Up the Flow of Information.   The speed of information transmission has transformed the world. For example, in 1845, it took 4 months for a single message to travel from New York to San Francisco, because the fastest means of communication was a clipper around Cape Horn.

Thirteen years later, the overland stagecoach reduced the time to 25 days. Two years later, in 1860, the same message took 10 days: The New York to Missouri telegraph followed by the St. Joseph to Sacramento pony express, delivered by steamship to San Francisco. The following year, the same message took only a few seconds with the completion of the coast-to-coast telegraph system.

Today, over 250,000 messages are sent over the same line, simultaneously, in a fraction of a second. Faster communications are helping businesses address complex problems, adapt to a constantly changing environment, and participate in the global marketplace.

6. Mass to Information Ratio Reversed.   Since the 1973 oil crisis, real or perceived, manufacturers have been forced to use more expensive energy to produce the same or better goods in order to maintain the American standard of living. To do this, more information per unit of production was used to make smarter products. Information, represented by the design, utility, or technology embedded into products, increased the effective use of mass production for goods.

The goal of the Information Age is simple: to do more for less. The products today must do more work for less money, use less energy, and require less labor.

The telephone is a product whose mass to information ratio is being reversed. Telephones now dial themselves; they remember; they compute; they record; they talk; they transmit voice, data, text, images, and video; they transfer money; they control energy and security; they are used in cars, planes, boats, and trains; they even fit into the decor.

The telephone's enhanced design and utility reduce the amount of labor and energy required to solve the problems of the marketplace.

7. Enhances Market Responsiveness.   Businesses are using telephone technology to increase the accessibility of their products and services in the marketplace. This is resulting in greater cost-effectiveness. Over $100 billion worth of products and services were exchanged in 1983 by telephone.

AT&T has tested the effectiveness of offering a prospective customer the option of returning a business reply card versus inquiring via an 800 number. Results show that total response from a mailing can be as much as 20 percent greater if both options are given. Furthermore, sales from telephone inquiries are up to four times greater than sales from mail inquiries.

8. Brings the Market to the Consumer.   The nature of the marketplace is changing again. Home delivery of products and services has returned. Phonebook-sized product catalogs and a nationwide network of distributors can deliver requests within a matter of hours of the phoned-in order.

Services vary from traditional floral deliveries to breakfast in bed, to liquor on Father's Day, to White Castle hamburgers 24 hours a day, to hypnosis for relaxation, to a market research report. Today, any service or product is as close as your telephone.

9. Consumer Controlled Delivery.   The consumer today is no longer dependent on the delivery schedule of those bringing the product or service to market. One rabbi offers teaching based on the Talmud to subscribers by taped messages, 24 hours a day. Businesspeople can listen to the teachings before beginning the workday or during a lunch break. A mother can study with the tape at her infant's nap time.

Shopping, horoscopes, betting, even counseling and medical services can be obtained at the time of need or the time of greatest convenience for the customer.

The pace of the marketplace is more than ever being dictated by the needs, wants, and desires of its customers. The ability to adapt to the schedules of working women, flex hours, and the impulsive nature of consumers offers a new set of challenges to businesses in the Information Age. No matter where you are in the world, by dialing one phone number you can receive any piece of information or product *when you want it.* As never before, the consumer is controlling delivery.

10. Integrates Electronic Payment.   Electronics and telecommunications are changing the way money is exchanged. The 976 telephone prefix is one service that is sparking the electronic payment revolution. Those three numbers are giving consumers access to a variety of specialized messages from stock market quotes to sports scores. What makes this service so appealing is that the call is charged to the caller's telephone and included in the phone company's regular billing cycle. After the customer pays the bill, the telephone company keeps its portion and remits the remainder to the vendor of the message. The telephone company does the collecting for the vendor.

A product that integrates electronic payment is a stock quotation service, which is available to anyone with a push-button phone. A deposit of $45 opens an account. The computer voice-synthesized "operator" gives the quote on any one of the 15,000 stocks, then deducts the charges from the account.

Another option for electronic transference of funds is quite easy to implement. Payment is made instantly over the phone by taking the name, credit card numbers, and expiration date of the bank or membership card, then verifying that it has not been lost or stolen.

THE NEW ECONOMIC ENVIRONMENT

The agrarian society began at the same time human beings emerged. The word *agrarian* connotes working of the soil to extract food and shelter from the land. The Civil War became a turning point in history by answering a basic question in the American culture: "Would the new continent be ruled by farmers or industrialists?"

The agricultural revolution introduced the industrial society. The cotton gin, which was invented in 1793, was one among many farm inventions that provided the impetus for the transition into the Industrial Age. The cotton gin featured a revolving brush that cleared the spikes and funneled seeds into another compartment. The key to Eli Whitney's invention was that it helped people do more work in less time. It simplified work by making large-scale production of cotton possible.

Soon after the invention of the cotton gin, cotton replaced tobacco as the leading plantation crop in the southern United States. The cotton gin, along with other inventions of new farm equipment, significantly improved agricultural production.

The cotton gin pointed the way for the farming culture to become a goods-producing economy. This led to assembly lines, mass distribution, corporations, big government, post offices, the producer-consumer relationship, and the widespread use of energy to produce and transport goods.

Certain assumptions were inherent in this new industrial economy:

- Nature is generous beyond limit.
- Industrial pursuits lead to social good.
- Economics is for the purpose of constant expansion.

Transportation, the hallmark of the industrial society, was a cost-effective way for people to communicate, entertain, and do business. Two events, however, would eventually change this forever. On October 4, 1957, the U.S.S.R. launched a space satellite called *Sputnik,* marking the beginning of the Space Age. The second event occurred on September 9, 1973, when the oil-exporting nations created an energy crisis through an oil embargo. The embargo spurred competition for limited resources and caused energy prices to soar. This had a dramatic impact on the energy-intensive transportation and goods-producing industries, which had consumed two-thirds of the world's oil and gas supplies between 1920 and 1970.

By increasing degrees in the years following *Sputnik* and the oil embargo, Americans began to sense some new harsh realities:

- Government could not solve all the problems.
- The myth of national omnipotence was shattered by Viet Nam.
- Individual security became more important than social reform.
- Political liberalism became equated with incompetence.
- Years of exponential expansion gave way to economic contractions.

These changes helped usher in the emerging social order known as the Information Age. At this time America began another large-scale shift—from a manufacturing economy to a service economy, dependent on science, information, and communication.

The shrinkage of America's manufacturing sector was mainly due to the depletion of its resource base, increases in the cost of energy, declines in productivity of capital-intensive industries, and downturns in the return on investment.

Although American manufacturing companies are setting up in third-world countries to capitalize on their minimal-cost labor pools, regulations, and taxes, and abundant supplies of energy, the growing American service sector still depends on manufacturing productivity at home.

In 1900, 30 percent of the labor force was service-oriented, while in 1980, 70 percent of the labor force was service-based. Today, the shrinkage of the manufacturing sector threatens to topple the service sector, since the service sector owes its very existence and vitality to a strong, healthy, capital-intensive manufacturing base.

Public services such as health care, education, transportation, and environmental care are dependent entirely on taxes. The energy crises, ecological disasters, inflation, and the downturn in manufacturing productivity have drained revenues earmarked for public services. Today, the average worker is less willing to be taxed, yet continues to expect and even demand greater public services.

Today, American employment is skewed as follows: 74 percent service-based, 23 percent manufacturing-based, and 3 percent agricultural-based. At the heart of this service-based economy is the information sector. The growth of the information sector was made possible by advances in computer information technology, most notably, the miniaturization of electronic computer components and chips. Yet, in order for information in the service sector to be productive, it requires delivery. And the most radical development to date in the field of information delivery is that of optical fibers. This innovation has increased information delivery capabilities almost 1000 times.

Information processing and delivery is altering the working environment and the economy. Up to 45 percent of service-sector jobs over the next 15 years will likely relate to information processing with half of these people working from their homes. Information delivery is at everyone's fingertips with 219 million business and residential phones alre dy in place. This infrastructure gives everyone instant accessibility to the information economy—a benefit to participants in the new economic environment.

The industrial economy focused on the use of energy, materials, and the embodied resources to produce a product or perform a service. This economy is being absorbed into one based on the changing ratio between the mass and the information contained in the goods and services.

Information in the new economy is represented by the knowledge and technology added to products and services. This embedded information makes products more useful and durable, easier to repair, stronger, and less energy consumptive.

The declining industrial economy is resulting from one important shift: changes in the ratio among labor (people), capital (money), and resources (energy). This shift began in 1973 when energy and capital rose in value (cost) while the value of a worker's time began to decline.

The goal of the industrial economy was to eliminate labor. Inexpensive energy fueled the machinery which did much of the industrial and agricultural work that people had performed. The industrial economy could not grow at its former rates because of the shifts in the ratio of values among labor, energy, and capital from the oil shocks. The structural foundations of the industrial economy had been shattered.

The information economy is not replacing the industrial economy. It is absorbing the industrial economy in the course of its evolution even with the recent downward turn in oil prices. The final shift into the information economy will be caused by a decline in the supply of resources rather than the result of a decline in the demand of products and services. The transition will reflect a shift in our national wealth—from mass and energy to information.

The emerging information economy is dictating how to respond to the new realities of the marketplace. This new economy is requiring labor and management, not just capital and energy, to bring value to products.

Manufacturers are being called on to create products with a higher ratio of information to materials. Small and medium-sized companies have been quick to respond. With better internal communications and an ability to change directions quickly, these entrepreneurial and innovative enterprises are creating products tailored to specific market needs.

The telephone is playing a significant role in this transformation. Telecommunications technologies help businesses do more work, using less energy, less manpower, and less capital to produce better products and greater profits.

To shift from the industrial economy to the information economy, technology must absorb industrial goods and make them more informational. In order for manufacturers to survive and thrive during this shift into the Information Age, they will need to integrate telephone technologies and creative techniques into the marketing mix: promotion, advertising, prospecting, selling, research, services, products, distribution, pricing and packaging—rapidly and thoroughly.

SUMMARY

Rather than establishing a set of concluding recommendations, I would like to invite you to sit in on a lecture to my students in small business management:

"Two final thoughts as we leave here today: Understand the lessons of history and learn the secrets of being a genius.

"History shows us that only about 5 percent of the population benefits directly and significantly from the upheaval that accompanies rapid technological change. You must be constantly asking yourselves what it takes to benefit from the current Information Revolution so you become part of the fortunate 5 percent.

"Another lesson history has taught us is the continual drive to do more for less. In 1776 America had 4 million farms which employed 90 percent of the labor force. One farmer could then feed 3 people. In 1980, there were 2.3 million farms which employed just 3 percent of the population. Yet one farmer could feed 77 people. Over the years technological advances have helped farmers do more work using fewer resources to produce more crops. Doing more work and producing better products that require less labor and fewer resources is a paradigm in today's business context.

"Where do you start? Start by observing how the telephone is changing the way business is being conducted. Telephone technologies are absorbing traditional marketing functions to produce more durable and efficient ways of satisfying the needs of the marketplace. New applications of the technology are emerging from the business marketing mix as the telephone is enhancing the synergistic effects of promotion, advertising, prospecting, selling, research, services, products, distribution, pricing, and packaging.

"By lowering the costs of doing business and speeding up the flow of information in the marketplace, the telephone will play an increasingly more important role in the future of your business success.

"The second thing you need to leave here with is the secret to being a genius: Becoming a bold person, making bold guesses, in anticipation of bold results. My view of genius is that it always begins with an idea. Geniuses often sacrifice themselves for their ideas and visions. When you get a good idea, let it *marinate*. Let what you do and read and think change you. Don't tell anybody about it. Let the idea become your own magnificent obsession.

"Next, *cogitate* on the idea. Toss your ideas around in your head, then pencil them out. Dream, imagine, speculate, research, develop, and design.

"From there, the idea will *impregnate*. Genius often erupts spontaneously when you are seeing and responding to a vision unavailable to the casual or critical observer. But this is only possible when you become dissatisfied with the way things are done and aim your dissent at finding a better way. Become a willing channel for an encounter with a timeless truth.

"The next phase is to *potentiate* the idea. Become like an electrical transformer—stepping down the staggering energy of the idea to a level commensurate with the world's capacity to see and use it.

"Finally, make decisions, not excuses. Be engaged in the process of seeking to be free from the limits of mediocrity. Establish a lifestyle conducive to inventiveness. Then your life will be enhanced and you will be a benefit to others."

Index